T0327919

DRAWINGS FROM THE GULAG

DRAWINGS AND TEXT Danzig Baldaev

DESIGN AND EDIT Murray & Sorrell FUEL
TRANSLATION Polly Gannon and Ast A. Moore
CO-ORDINATOR Julia Goumen

Drawings from the Gulag

FUEL

Danzig Baldaev was born in 1925 in Ulan-Ude, Buryatiya, Russia. The son of an 'enemy of the people', he was subject to repression in Communist Russia and sent to an orphanage for children of political prisoners. After serving in the army during the Second World War, he came to Leningrad in 1948 and was ordered by the NKVD to work as a warden in Kresty – an infamous prison – where he started drawing the tattoos of criminals. He was reported to the KGB who unexpectedly supported him, realising the status of a criminal could be determined by deciphering the meaning of his tattoos. His work enabled him to visit different reformatory settlements across the former USSR, where he witnessed many of the scenes published in this book.

Contents

All footnotes have been researched and written by the editors. Quotes from various sources have been used where appropriate to corroborate the author's drawings and text (all sources are credited at the end of each quote).

Damon Murray, Stephen Sorrell

The drawings in this book reveal an episode of the most horrific suffering in the life of a country that is known for its capacity to endure suffering.

Initially they appear over-dramatic, focusing on the abject, the grotesque and the aberrant. Perhaps because they aren't photographs it is easier to dismiss them as a figment of a disturbed imagination. But even a basic reading of the literature concerning this period reveals that they are undeniably 'factual' drawings. There is a disturbed imagination at work here, but it belongs to the interrogator, the guard and the criminal. Although these interpretations of Gulag scenes are drawn by an artist, and retain the unmistakable identity of his hand, Baldaev has resisted pictorial flourishes, communicating his views in a direct and unswerving way. Where Gulag literature uses a turn of phrase or metaphor to help us imagine its surreal horror and give us an emotional understanding, Baldaev's harsh, vernacular drawings tell the story using a straightforward, unremittingly brutal method, faithful to the system he was attempting to document.

Obviously no one could be present at all the events shown in this book. Baldaev's widow has explained how around a fifth of the drawings are from first-hand experience. The rest of the images are the result of the artist's meticulous research, speaking to fellow NKVD officers and prisoners about particular incidents, practises and procedures. He wanted the drawings to be accurate in every detail, from a slogan on a placard, to a collar on a uniform. His father was an ethnographer who had been arrested as an 'enemy of the people' and sent to the Gulag, while Baldaev and his sister were sent to an orphanage for Family Members of Enemies of the People. It is impossible to gauge the effect such events might have on a child, but through this work it is clear that, despite becoming part of the system, he wanted to expose the lie behind it. He soaked up the evidence before him and committed it to paper, spending twenty years working at home, in secret, on these drawings. If he had been discovered he would certainly have suffered the same fate as the Gulag victims he so assiduously depicted.

In his book *Kolyma Tales*, referring to the terrible sights he and his fellow inmates witnessed, Varlam Shalamov wrote, 'A human being survives by his ability to forget.' These events are not as well known as they should be. Perhaps that has something to do with survival – which in its own way carries a particular sense of guilt. Values change in the Gulag. Reduced to their basic functions, one emaciated inmate looks much like another, harder to recognise as an individual, less than a human being, disposable. *Drawings from the Gulag* makes explicit the capacity one individual has to destroy another. It shows how moral borders disintegrate, and how the descent into indifference can be sanctioned, justified and excused in pursuit of a flawed ideology.

Birth of the Gulag

ЗАЧАТИЕ ГУЛАГА
ВПЕРЕД ЗАРЕ НАВСТРЕЧУ, ТОВАРИЩИ, ДРУЗЬЯ!...

ДОЛОЙ ЦАРЯ!

ВСЯ СО

НАЧАЛО ПУТИ В КОММУНИСТИЧЕСКОЕ (СТАЛИНСКОЕ) РАБСТВО— ГУЛАГ ГПУ-НКВД-МВ

Text top left reads: 'The Inception of the Gulag.* Go Forth Toward the Dawn, Comrades and Friends!'; text top right reads: 'Dedicated to the 70th anniversary of the giant of Russian literature, A.I. Solzhenitsyn. 11th November 1988. [signature] Danzig Baldaev'. Text on the left banner reads: 'Down with the Czar!'; text on the centre banner reads: 'All Power to the Soviets!'; text on the right reads: '25th October (7th November [o.s.†]) 1917'.

The beginning of the road to Communist (Stalin) bondage: Gulag, GPU-NKVD-MVD.‡
(Shortly thereafter, the peoples of Russia recalled life under the czar as a lost paradise.)

Посвещается 70-летию колосса
русской литературы А.И.Солженицину
11.XI.1988г. *Балдаев*   Д.С.Балдаев

ЧЕРЕЗ КОРОТКОЕ ВРЕМЯ НАРОДЫ РОССИИ ВСПОМИНАЛИ ЖИЗНЬ ПРИ ЦАРЕ КАК ОБ УТРАЧЕННОМ РАЕ...)

* Gulag or GULAG (*Glavnoye Upravleniye Ispravitelno-Trudovikh Lageryey i Koloniy*) – the Chief Administration of Corrective Labour Camps and Colonies.
† o.s. (Old Style) or Julian calendar is used to refer to dates from czarist times, Russia switched to the Gregorian calendar in 1918.
‡ GPU (*Gosudarstvennoye Politicheskoye Upravlenie*) – the State Political Directorate of the NKVD of the RSFSR. The secret police of the Soviet Union from 1922 until 1934.
NKVD (*Narodnyy Komissariat Vnutrennikh Del*) – the People's Commissariat for Internal Affairs. The civilian and secret police of the Soviet Union during the era of Stalin.
MVD (*Ministerstvo Vnutrennikh Del*) – the Ministry of Internal Affairs. First formed in czarist Russia in 1802. Re-established in 1990.

РОЖДЕНИЕ Г
И КРАСНОГО

По Декрету от 5.9.18 г. ВЧК ПОЛУЧИЛА НЕ ОГРАНИЧЕННЫЕ ПРАВА НА
КИМ МЕТОДОМ УБЕЖДЕНИЙ" И РАССТРЕЛОВ БЫЛИ УНИЧТОЖЕНЫ
И ТОЛЬКО ПУТЁМ ЖЕСТОЧАЙШЕГО ТЕРРОРА КОММУНИСТЫ УДЕ

The Birth of the Gulag and Red Terror. September 5th, 1918.
Writing on the wall: **'The Solovki Prison Camp.* USLON† OGPU‡'**.

The decree of 5th September 1918 gave the VChK§ an unrestricted right to claim the lives and freedoms of the citizens of the country. Over a short period, using 'methods of physical persuasion' and execution, over 500,000 people were killed, and hundreds of thousands more were placed in prison camps. Only through the most brutal terror and repression of the people were the Communists able to retain their power.

СВОБОДУ ГРАЖДАН СТРАНЫ. ЗА КОРОТКИЙ ПЕРИОД „ФИЗИЧЕС-
500 ТЫС.ЧЕЛОВЕК И СОТНИ ТЫСЯЧ ПОМЕЩЕНЫ В КОНЦЛАГЕРЯ.
СВОЮ АНТИНАРОДНУЮ ВЛАСТЬ...

* Many monasteries were easily adapted into labour camps and prisons by the authorities, their construction lending themselves to this purpose. The Solovki Monastery was converted into the infamous *Solovetsky Lager Osobogo Naznachenia* (Solovki Special Purpose Camp) or SLON (an acronym meaning 'elephant' in Russian). Solzhenitsyn called it the 'mother of the Gulag'.

† USLON *Upravlenie Solovetskimi Lageryami Osobogo Naznacheniya* – the Directorate of Solovki Special Prison Camps.

‡ OGPU *Obyedinennoe Gosudarstvennoe Politicheskoe Upravlenie* – the Joint State Political Directorate (also known as the All-Union State Political Administration). Formed after the GPU left the NKVD in 1923.

§ VChK *Vserossiyskaya Chrezvychainaya Komissiya* – the All-Russian Extraordinary Commission [for Combating Counter revolution and Sabotage] or Cheka. The first in a series of state security organisations responsible for enforcing the will of the Communist government. Their tasks ranged from the requisition of food to the execution of political opponents.

По указанию „вождя люмпиков" В.Ленина...

В НАЧАЛЕ 20-Х ГОДОВ В Г. ВЛАДИКАВКАЗЕ ВЧК БЫЛИ АРЕСТОВАНЫ СВЯ-
ЩЕННОСЛУЖИТЕЛИ РАЗНЫХ ВЕРОИСПОВЕДАНИЙ, КОТОРЫМ ПЕРЕД РАС-
СТРЕЛОМ ПРЕДЛОЖИЛИ ОТКАЗАТЬСЯ ОТ РЕЛИГИИ, ДЛЯ СОХРАНЕНИЯ СВО-
ЕЙ ЖИЗНИ. БЫЛ ОТ ВСЕХ ПОЛУЧЕН ОТКАЗ. МОЛОДОЙ ЛЮТЕРАНСКИЙ СВЯ-
ЩЕННИК ПЛЮНУЛ В ЛИЦО КОМИССАРУ. ВСЕ ОНИ ПРИНЯЛИ СМЕРТЬ С БОЛЬ-
ШИМ ДОСТОИНСТВОМ И СПОКОЙСТВИЕМ, ДАВ ПРИМЕР ДРУГИМ...

By order of the 'lumpen-proletariat leader,' Vladimir Lenin . . .

In the early 1920s in Vladikavkaz, the VChK arrested priests of various religious faiths and denominations. Before execution, they were given the choice to deny their religion in exchange for their lives. All of them refused. A young Lutheran priest spat in the face of one Commissar. They accepted death calmly and with dignity, setting an example for others.

– ЕСЛИ ТВОЯ БАНДА ПОПОВ-ВРАГОВ МАРКСИЗМА, РАНЕЕ ДУРМА-
НИВШАЯ НАРОД ОБЕЩАНИЕМ РАЯ, НЕ БУДЕТ ВЫПОЛНЯТЬ НОР-
МУ ПО СТРОИТЕЛЬСТВУ КОММУНИЗМА-СВЕТЛОГО БУДУЩЕГО
ДЛЯ ТРУДОВОГО НАРОДА, Я ВАС ПЕРЕСТРЕЛЯЮ КАК ЧЕРТЕЙ
И САБОТАЖНИКОВ!

'If your gang of priests – enemies of Marxism who tricked the people with false promises of heaven – don't meet the quota for building Communism and the bright future of the working class, I'll shoot you all like saboteurs, you devils!'

Text across the top reads: **'Long Live the Communist Party, the Wisest of the Wise, Whose Wisdom Outwitted the Wisdom of Wisdom Itself! Glory to the RKP(b)-VKP(b)-KPSS!**'; text across the bottom reads: **'Down with churches, monasteries, Roman Catholic, Lutheran, and others! Religion is the drug of the people. Priests and monks are the worst enemies of Soviet power!'**.

Over 100,000 Christian churches, around 20,000 Muslim mosques, 500 Buddhist datsans and 1,400 synagogues were destroyed during the Soviet era. Over 450,000 priests and millions of believers were killed. People were disconnected from their cultures, cultures were suppressed, and the moral lives of the citizens of the country were deformed and distorted.

И, КОСТЕЛЫ, КИРХИ, ХРАМЫ!
И ЗЛОБНЫЕ ВРАГИ СОВЕТСКОЙ ВЛАСТИ!

ЬМАНСКИХ МЕЧЕТЕЙ, 500 БУДДИЙСКИХ ДАЦАНОВ, 1400 ИУДЕЙСКИХ СИНАГОГ. ИСТРЕБЛЕНО ФИЗИЧЕСКИ
РЫ, ОБЕСКУЛЬТУРИВАНИЕ И ДЕФОРМАЦИЯ НРАВСТВЕННОГО ВОСПИТАНИЯ ГРАЖДАН СТРАНЫ...
ЫБЛЕЙ ИМУЩЕСТВО И ДРАГОЦЕННОСТИ ПО СМЕХОТВОРНОЙ ЦЕНЕ БЫЛИ ПРОДАНЫ КОММУНИСТАМИ ЗА РУБЕЖ...

From the Civil War (1917–1922) onward, Churches and monasteries were raided by order of Vladimir Lenin.
The Communists sold off the property and valuables, worth billions of rubles, for almost nothing to buyers abroad.

* Throughout the years, the Communist Party went through several official names:
RKP(b) (*Rossiyskaya Kommunisticheskaya Partiya (bolshevikov)*) – the Russian Communist Party (of Bolsheviks), 1918-1925.
VKP(b) (*Vsesoyuznaya Kommunisticheskaya Partiya (bolshevikov)*) – the All-Union Communist Party (of Bolsheviks), 1925-1952.
KPSS (*Kommunisticheskaya Partiya Sovetskogo Soyuza*) – the Communist Party of the Soviet Union, 1952-1991 (dissolved).

Arrest, Interrogation and Imprisonment

– НАМ ПО РАЗНАРЯДКЕ НУЖНО ПРИВЕЗТИ 12 ВРАГОВ, С ЭТИМИ ИНЖЕ-
НЕРОМ, ВРАЧИХОЙ И СТАРЫМ КОЗЛОМ, ПРОФЕССОРОМ, НАБИРАЕТСЯ
ВСЕГО 10, ТОГДА ЗАБЕРИТЕ ИЗ КВАРТИР ПЕРВОГО ЭТАЖА ЕЩЕ ЛЮ-
БЫХ ДВУХ, КТО ТАМ ЕСТЬ, РАБОЧИЙ-КОЛХОЗНИК, ВСЕ РАВНО, ЛИШЬ БЫ
БЫЛ ПОЛНЫМ СЧЁТ-12! ИСПОЛНЯЙТЕ!...

Writing on the van: **'NKVD*'**.

'We've been instructed to round up twelve enemies [of the people]. With the engineer, the doctor woman and the old moron professor, we've only got ten. Take any two people from the apartments on the first floor, whoever you can get – workers or *kolkhozniks*† – it doesn't matter. We just need twelve people in all. That's an order. Off you go…'

* The NKVD vans were rarely marked in this way, often bread or milk vans were used to disguise their real purpose.
† The farmer of a kolkhoz (*kollektivnoe khzyaistvo*) – collective farm.

ОДИН ИЗ „ГУМАННЫХ" МЕТОДОВ НКВД-„ВЫТЯНУТЬ"
НУЖНЫЕ ПОКАЗАНИЯ У ЗЭКА-„ВРАГА НАРОДА"...

РАБОТНИКИ НКВД ПРЕДВАРИТЕЛЬНО ЖЕРТВУ ДОЛГО МОРИЛИ ГОЛОДОМ И ЗАТЕМ
НА ДОПРОСЕ „ВРАГУ НАРОДА" ПРЕДЛАГАЛИ ОБИЛЬНОЕ УГОЩЕНИЕ ЗА ДАЧУ НУЖ-
НЫХ ПОКАЗАНИЙ НА СЕБЯ ИЛИ ДРУГОЕ ЛИЦО. БЫЛ И ДРУГОЙ МЕТОД, КОГДА
ЖЕРТВУ КОРМИЛИ СОЛЁНОЙ ПИЩЕЙ И 2-3 ДНЯ НЕ ДАВАЛИ ВОДЫ, КРОМЕ
СОЛЁНОЙ БАЛАНДЫ, И ТОЛЬКО НА ДОПРОСЕ ДАВАЛИ ВОДУ ЗА „ПОКАЗАНИЯ"...

One of the more 'humane' methods employed by the NKVD to 'extract' the necessary statement from an 'enemy of the people'.*

The NKVD starved the victim for a long time. Then, during the interrogation, the 'enemy of the people' was offered a hearty meal in exchange for the desired statement against himself or a denunciation. Another method involved feeding the victim food with a high salt content, then depriving them of water for two or three days. The only liquid available was the *balanda* (prison soup), which was also over-salted. Water was given only during interrogations in exchange for a forced statement.

* Used by Lenin as early as the decree of 28th November 1917, the phrase 'enemy of the people', was a loose term that could be applied to anyone the authorities conceived as a threat. 'Enemies of the people' were imprisoned, expelled or executed. Their relatives and friends also fell under suspicion and could be sent to the Gulag as 'Family Members of Traitors of the Motherland'.

-ТВОЙ МУЖ, БЫВШИЙ КОМАНДИР ДИВИЗИИ, РАССТРЕЛЯН, КАК ВРАГ... ПРИХОД СВЭ И ЧСИР НА РЕГИСТРАЦИЮ В ОРГАНЫ НКВД-МВД... ЭТО БЫЛИ РОДСТВЕННИКИ „ВРАГОВ НАРОДА", СОСЛАННЫЕ БЕЗ СУДА И СЛЕДСТВИЯ В СЕВЕРНЫЕ И ВОСТОЧНЫЕ РАЙОНЫ, ГДЕ ЖИЛИ В ХОЛОДЕ И ГОЛОДЕ И УМИРАЛИ ТЫСЯЧАМИ...

Sign on the wall reads: **'Death to the Class Enemy!'**.

'Your husband, a former Division Commander, was executed as an enemy of the people.'
'Family Members of Traitors of the Motherland' and the 'Socially Dangerous'* had to register with the NKVD-MVD. These were relatives of the 'enemies of the people', exiled without trial to the northern and north-eastern regions. They lived there in conditions of cold and hunger and died by the thousands.

* Regular citizens were most likely to be arrested for these two 'offences'. However, undesirables could be imprisoned under many different charges. The titles of some of these 'crimes': 'counter-revolutionary thinking', 'praising American technology', 'holding anti-Soviet moods'; reveal the level of paranoia within the authorities themselves.

НКВД ПОКРЫЛО СТРАНУ ГУСТОЙ ПАУЧЬЕЙ СЕТЬЮ ДОНОСЧИКОВ- „СТУКАЧАМИ" И „СЕКСОТАМИ" (СЕКРЕТНЫМИ СОТРУДНИКАМИ)...

ТАЙНАЯ СЕТЬ ДОНОСЧИКОВ ДЕРЖАЛА ВЕСЬ НАРОД В СМЕРТЕЛЬНОМ СТРАХЕ, КАК ВО ВРЕМЕНА СРЕДНЕВЕКОВОЙ ИНКВИЗИЦИИ. „СТУКАЧИ" ЛЮДИ БЕЗ ЧЕСТИ, СТЫДА И СОВЕСТИ, БЫЛИ АКТИВОМ НКВД. ОНИ ИЗ ЛИЧНОЙ КОРЫСТИ, ЧЕРНОЙ ЗАВИСТИ И ДРУГИХ НИЗМЕННЫХ ПОБУЖДЕНИЙ, УСТНО И ПИСЬМЕННО ДОНОСИЛИ НА РОДНЫХ, БЛИЗ-КИХ, ДРУЗЕЙ, ТОВАРИЩЕЙ, ЗНАКОМЫХ, ОДНОКАМЕРНИКОВ И ОБВИНЯЛИ ИХ ВО ВСЕХ СМЕРТНЫХ ГРЕХАХ: В ШПИОНАЖЕ, ВРЕ-ДИТЕЛЬСТВЕ, ЗАГОВОРЕ, АНТИСОВЕТСКОЙ АГИТАЦИИ И Т.Д.
    НИКАКОЙ ПРОВЕРКИ НКВД В ПРАВДИВОСТИ ДОНОСОВ НЕ ПРОВОДИЛ, А НАОБОРОТ ПООЩРЯЛ ЛЮБУЮ ЧУДОВИЩНУЮ ЛОЖЬ...

The NKVD covered the country with a dense network of narks and secret informers.

The secret informer network kept the entire population in deathly fear, akin to that of the Inquisition. Informants,* people with no feelings, honour, or remorse, were a valuable asset of the NKVD. Out of a sense of profit, greed, envy and other brute instincts, they reported – orally or in writing – on their friends, relatives, immediate family, acquaintances, and fellow inmates. They accused them of all the deadly sins: espionage, sabotage, conspiracy, anti-Soviet propaganda and agitation, etc. The NKVD never verified the informants' reports. On the contrary, it encouraged the most blatant lies.

* 'In the 1930s, Nadezhda Mandelstam tells us, the verb *to write* assumed a new meaning. When you said *he writes* or *does she write?* or (referring to a whole classroom of students) *they write*, you meant that he or she or they *wrote reports to the organs*. (Similarly, the Cheka's rigged cases were called "novels".) To "write" meant to inform, to denounce. Solzhenitsyn calls it "murder by slander".' Martin Amis, *Koba the Dread*, 2002.

МЛАДШИЙ КРОВАВЫЙ БРАТ НКВД-ГЕСТАПО ТАК И НЕ ДОРОС ДО „ВСЕНАРОДНОГО ГНЕВНОГО ОСУЖДЕНИЯ ВРАГОВ ФАТЕРЛЯНДА" И БЕСКОНЕЧНО ОТСТАВАЛ ПО „ПРОИЗВОДИТЕЛЬНОСТИ ТРУДА"...

ПО УКАЗКЕ НКВД НА ЗАВОДАХ, ФАБРИКАХ, В КОЛХОЗАХ, НАУЧНЫХ, УЧЕБНЫХ ЗАВЕДЕНИЯХ И УЧРЕЖДЕНИЯХ ПО ВСЕЙ СТРАНЕ ПРОВОДИЛИСЬ СОБРАНИЯ ТРУДЯЩИХСЯ, ГДЕ ВЫСТУПАЮЩИЕ КЛЕЙМИЛИ ПОЗОРОМ „ШПИОНОВ, ДИВЕРСАНТОВ, ВРЕДИТЕЛЕЙ, ЗАВЕРБОВАННЫХ ИНОСТРАННЫМИ РАЗВЕДКАМИ," ОБЕЗВРЕЖЕННЫХ НКВД, И ТРЕБОВАЛИ ИХ УНИЧТОЖЕНИЯ, КАК „БЕШЕНЫХ СОБАК." МНОГИЕ ВЫСТУПАВШИЕ НА ЭТИХ СОБРАНИЯХ И МИТИНГАХ ВСКОРЕ САМИ ОКАЗЫВАЛИСЬ НА ПОЛОЖЕНИИ „БЕШЕНЫХ СОБАК" И ШЛИ ПОД РАССТРЕЛ...

The Gestapo, the bloody younger brother of the NKVD, never matured enough to adopt the notion of 'universal wrathful condemnation of the enemies of the Fatherland', and it lagged far behind in terms of 'labour efficiency'.

By order of the NKVD, workers' meetings were held at factories, plants, kolkhozes, scientific institutes and educational institutions throughout the country. At these meetings people took the stage to publicly condemn 'spies, wreckers, and saboteurs in the pay of international intelligence', who had been exposed by the NKVD. They demanded they be exterminated 'like a pack of wild dogs'. Many of those who stood on the podium soon became part of the pack 'wild dogs' themselves, and were executed by firing squad.[*]

[*]During Stalin's many purges some of his most loyal followers fell victim to his deadly paranoia. His ruthless cleansing of (mostly imagined) political opposition, was a constant feature of his regime. No one was immune, including those who had previously denounced others. 'We think that a powerful and vigorous movement is impossible without differences – "true conformity" is possible only in the cemetery.' Joseph Stalin, 'Our purposes', *Pravda*, 22 January 1912.

ДОПРОС ДЕТЕЙ „ВРАГОВ НАРОДА" О КОНТРРЕВОЛЮ-ЦИОННОЙ ДЕЯТЕЛЬНОСТИ ИХ РОДИТЕЛЕЙ И БЛИЗКИХ...

СТАЛИНСКИЙ НКВД ПООЩРЯЛ ДОНОСЫ ДЕТЕЙ НА СВОИХ РОДИТЕЛЕЙ И ВОЗВОДИЛ ИХ В ГЕРОИ, А НЕКОТОРЫХ ИЗБИЕНИЕМ ЗАСТАВЛЯЛ ДАВАТЬ НУЖНЫЕ ПОКАЗАНИЯ. ПО СТРАНЕ ПРОШЛА КАМПАНИЯ ПУБЛИЧНОГО ОТРЕЧЕНИЯ ДЕТЕЙ ОТ СВОИХ РОДИТЕЛЕЙ-ВРАГОВ НАРОДА", ЧЕРЕЗ ГАЗЕТЫ ИХ ЗАСТАВЛЯЛИ ВЫСТУПАТЬ НА СОБРАНИЯХ „С ГНЕВНЫМ ОСУЖДЕНИЕМ ШПИОНОВ И Т.Д." НЕКОТОРЫЕ УЧИТЕЛЯ ШКОЛ ПРЕДЛАГАЛИ ПИСАТЬ СОЧИНЕНИЯ-„ЧТО ДУМАЕТЕ ВЫ (УЧЕНИКИ) И ВАШИ ОТЕЦ И МАТЬ ОБ АРЕСТЕ МАРШАЛОВ СССР БЛЮХЕРА, ТУХАЧЕВСКОГО, ЕГОРОВА И ДР.?" И ПОСЛЕ ТАКИХ „СОЧИНЕНИЙ" МНОГИЕ ЛИШАЛИСЬ РОДИТЕЛЕЙ И НАПРАВЛЯЛИСЬ В ДЕТДОМА „ЧС"...

The interrogation of children of the 'enemies of the people' about the contra-revolutionary activities of their parents and close relatives.

Stalin's NKVD encouraged children to denounce their parents. Some were held up as heroes;[*] others were tortured to make them 'confess'. A campaign of public denunciations by children of their 'enemies of the people' elders was launched countrywide. Through newspapers, children were ordered to make public speeches and 'wrathfully condemn spies', etc. Some schoolteachers assigned students essays on subjects such as 'What do you (the student) and your father and mother think about the arrest of Marshals Tukhachevsky, Blücher, Egorov,[†] and others?' As a result of these 'essays', many children became orphans and were sent to special ChS (*chlen semyi* – member of the family [of the enemy of the people]) orphanages.[‡]

[*] Pavel (Pavlik) Morozov was the most famous example of this phenomenon. In 1932, following his denunciation of his father, thirteen-year-old Pavlik was murdered by enraged family members. He was exalted as an icon of integrity: someone who held the values of the state higher than family love. Idolised in propaganda: schools, streets and pioneer brigades were named after him. His story was a parable for generations of Soviet children. Recent investigations have cast considerable doubt on the official version of events. In her book *Comrade Pavlik* (2005), Catriona Kelly argues the case had been almost entirely constructed to suit the political doctrine of the time.
[†] Marshal Mikhail Tukhachevsky and eight other higher military commanders were convicted and executed in 1937 after a secret trial known as 'The Case of Trotskyist Anti-Soviet Military Organisation'. Marshal Vasily Blücher was arrested in 1938 and convicted of spying for Japan. Marshal Alexander Egorov was demoted to Commander at the end of 1937 and then arrested in 1938. He died in prison in 1939 (or 1941, according to some sources). Both Egorov and Blücher were members of the tribunal that convicted Tukhachevsky.
[‡] Baldaev and his younger sister were both placed in an orphanage for children of 'enemies of the people' following their father's arrest.

НА ДОПРОСАХ „ВРАГОВ НАРОДА" ШИРОКО ПРИМЕНЯЛСЯ ПРИЁМ – „СТОЙКА МОРДОЙ В УГОЛ, РУКИ ПО ШВАМ"...

ЖЕРТВЫ НКВД-МГБ-МВД „ВРАГИ НАРОДА" СТОЯЛИ НА ДОПРОСАХ ПО НЕСКОЛЬКО СУТОК БЕЗ СНА, ВОДЫ, ПИЩИ, ОТДЫХА. ПРИ ПАДЕНИИ ОТ ПОТЕРИ СИЛ ЖЕРТВУ ОБЛИВАЛИ ВОДОЙ, ИЗБИВАЛИ И СНОВА СТАВИЛИ В УГОЛ. ПАЛАЧИ ЗА СВОЁ УСЕРДИЕ НАГРАЖДАЛИСЬ ОРДЕНАМИ И С ПОЧЁТОМ ВЫШЛИ В ОТСТАВКУ В 50-60 ГОДАХ...

Another method of torture during interrogations: 'Stand facing the corner, hands by your sides...'
Text on the left wall reads: **'The goal of the ChK* is to fight class enemies mercilessly'**; text above the door reads: **'Long Live Comrade Stalin!'**; portrait above the map: Felix Dzerzhinsky;[†] text on the map reads: **'Administr[ation]'**.

Victims of the NKVD-MVD, 'the enemies of the people' were made to stand up for days during interrogations. They went without sleep, water, food, or rest. When they fainted, water was poured over them, then they were beaten and forced to stand in the corner again. For their diligence, the executors were awarded medals, and retired 'with honours' in the 1950s and 1960s.

* The Cheka (see VChK, page 14).
† Felix Dzerzhinsky, 'Iron Felix' founder of the Cheka and later head of the GPU .

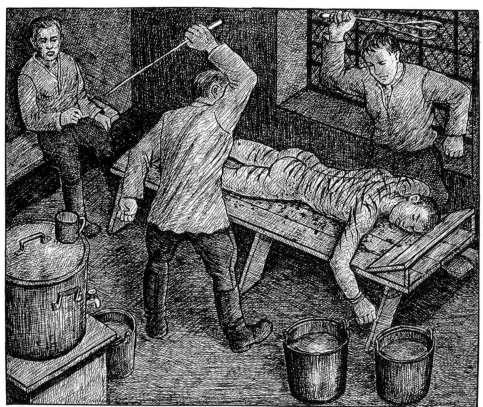

— ЕГО ПОРА ОБЛИТЬ ВОДОЙ. ЭТОТ КЛАССОВЫЙ ВРАГ УЖЕ ПОНЯЛ, ЧТО ТАКОЕ ПРОЛЕТАРСКАЯ ДИКТАТУРА, ГПУ, КОЛЛЕКТИВИЗАЦИЯ И „КОЛХОЗ ДЕЛО-ДОБРОВОЛЬНОЕ"...

'Time to pour water over him. This class enemy already understands what the dictatorship of the proletariat, the GPU, collectivization and 'the kolkhoz is a voluntary act' are all about.'

* 'The investigators began to use force on me, a sick, sixty-five-year-old man. I was made to lie face down and then beaten on the soles of my feet and my spine with a rubber strap. They sat me on a chair and beat my feet from above, with considerable force… For the next few days, when those parts of my legs were covered with extensive internal haemorrhaging, they again beat the red-blue-and-yellow bruises with the strap and the pain was so intense it felt as if boiling hot water was being poured on these sensitive areas. I howled and wept from the pain. They beat my back with the same rubber strap and punched my face, swinging their fists from a great height. The intolerable physical and emotional pain caused my eyes to weep unending streams of tears. Lying face down on the floor, I discovered that I could wriggle, twist and squeal like a dog when its master whips it. One time my body was shaking so uncontrollably that the guard escorting me back from such an interrogation asked: "Have you got malaria?" When I lay down on the cot and fell asleep, after eighteen hours of interrogation, in order to go back in an hour's time for more, I was woken up by my own groaning and because I was jerking about like a patient in the last stages of typhoid fever. Constantly the interrogator repeated, threateningly, "If you won't write (invent, in other words?!) then we shall beat you again, leaving your head and your right arm untouched but reducing the rest to a hacked, bleeding and shapeless body." So I signed everything.' An extract from a letter dated 13th January 1940, sent to Vyacheslav Molotov (head of the Sovnarkom, the administrative arm of the Soviet government), by the seminal theatre director and producer Vsevelod Meyerhold, complaining about his treatment at the hands of his interrogators. He was executed by firing squad on 2nd February 1940.

В ОДНОЙ ИЗ МНОГОЧИСЛЕННЫХ ТЮРЕМ НКВД – „ВЕДУТ" ПОС-
ЛЕ ОЧЕРЕДНОГО ДОПРОСА 3-Й СТЕПЕНИ „ВРАГА НАРОДА"...

СТАЛИНСКИЙ НКВД САМЫМИ ДИКИМИ, ЗВЕРСКИМИ СРЕДНЕВЕКОВЫ-
МИ ПЫТКАМИ ВЫБИВАЛ У СОВЕРШЕННО НЕВИННЫХ ЛЮДЕЙ САМЫЕ
ФАНТАСТИЧЕСКИЕ ПРИЗНАНИЯ – „ШПИОНАЖ В ПОЛЬЗУ БУРЖУАЗ-
НОГО ГОСУДАРСТВА АНТАРКТИДЫ"...

The 'enemy of the people' is being 'led away' after a third degree interrogation session in one of the many prisons of the **NKVD**.

Using the most vile and inhumane forms of torture, akin to those of the Middle Ages, the Stalinist NKVD forced innocent people to make the most ridiculous and outrageous 'confessions', such as 'spying for the bourgeois state of Antarctica'.

РАБОТНИКИ НКВД ПРИ ДОПРОСАХ „ВРАГОВ НАРОДА" ПРИМЕНЯЛИ СТАРОРУССКУЮ ПЫТКУ – ДЫБУ...

Узаконенный И.Сталиным и Генеральным прокурором СССР А.Вышинск-им, допрос 3-й степени позволял выколачивать любые показания у „врага народа" на себя и других лиц, и многие, чтобы избавить себя от дальнейших пыток, „признавались" в шпионаже, диверсии, загово-ре и т.д., сознательно шли под расстрел в убойном цехе УФУ НКВД...

One of the instruments of torture that the NKVD used during interrogations of 'enemies of the people' was the rack, which dates back many centuries in Russia.

The 'third degree interrogation', legalised by Joseph Stalin and the General Prosecutor of the USSR, Andrey Vyshinsky, made it possible to obtain any statements from the 'enemies of the people' against themselves or others. In order to avoid further torture, many 'confessed' to espionage, sabotage, conspiracy, etc., preferring execution by firing squad in the 'slaughterhouse' of the UFU* NKVD.

* UFU (*Upravlenie Fizicheskogo Unichtozheniya*) – the Department of Physical Extermination.

ДЛЯ ПСИХИЧЕСКОГО ВОЗДЕЙСТВИЯ НА ДОПРОСАХ ЖЕН-ЩИН И ДЕВУШЕК „ВРАГОВ НАРОДА" РАЗДЕВАЛИ ДОГОЛА...

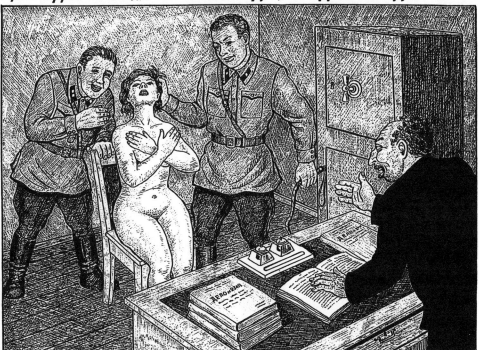

РАБОТНИКИ НКВД ИЗ КАТЕГОРИИ „СЕКСУАЛЬНО ОЗАБОЧЕННЫХ" БЫЛИ БОЛЬШИМИ ЛЮБИТЕЛЯМИ НА ДОПРОСАХ РАЗДЕВАТЬ ДОНАГА МОЛОДЫХ ЖЕНЩИН И ОСОБЕННО ДЕВУШЕК ИЗ КОНТИНГЕНТА „ВРАГОВ НАРОДА" И ИХ „ЧС", Т.Е. ЧЛЕНОВ СЕМЕЙ. УСТНЫЕ И ПИСЬМЕННЫЕ ЖАЛОБЫ О ПЫТКАХ, ИСТЯЗАНИЯХ, ИЗНАСИЛОВАНИЯХ И ИЗДЕВАТЕЛЬСТВАХ ВЛАСТЯМИ НЕ ПРИНИМАЛИСЬ. ЧЕСТНЫЕ И ПРИНЦИПИАЛЬНЫЕ РАБОТНИКИ ПРОКУРАТУРЫ БЫЛИ ИСТРЕБЛЕНЫ. НКВД ИМЕЛ НЕОГРАНИЧЕННЫЕ ПРАВА НА ЖИЗНЬ ВСЕХ ГРАЖДАН СТРАНЫ, А ПРОКУРАТУРА СТАЛА БЕСПРАВНОЙ МАРИОНЕТКОЙ И ПОСОБНИЦЕЙ НКВД...

A form of psychological pressure: women and girls, 'enemies of the people', were stripped naked during interrogation.

'Sexually preoccupied' employees of the NKVD were very keen on stripping young women[*] – 'enemies of the people' or the members of their families – during interrogations. Oral or written complaints about torture, rape, or humiliation were rejected by the authorities. Honest employees and men of principle who worked in prosecution were exterminated. The NKVD had unlimited rights to claim the lives of any citizen of the country. The public prosecutor's office became the NKVD's puppet and accomplice.

[*] '… you are interrogating a "foreigner's girlfriend"… all of a sudden you get an idea: maybe she learned something from those foreigners… And so you begin to interrogate her energetically: *How?* What positions? More! In detail! …The girl is blushing and in tears. "It doesn't have anything to do with the case," she protests. "Yes, it does, speak up!" That's power for you! She gives you the full details. If you want she'll draw a picture for you. If you want she'll demonstrate with her body. She has no way out. In your hands you hold the punishment cell and her *prison term.*' Aleksandr Solzhenitsyn, *The Gulag Archipelago*, 1973.

-ТЫ ПРОБРАЛСЯ В ЖЕЛЕЗНЫЕ РЯДЫ НКВД, ЧТОБЫ СПАСАТЬ АРЕСТОВАННЫХ ВРАГОВ НАРОДА И РАЗНУЮ СВОЛОЧЬ...

Background picture: Vladimir Lenin giving his famous speech at the Finland Station, Petrograd (now St. Petersburg), following his return from exile in April 1917.

'You have infiltrated the steely ranks of the NKVD to save imprisoned enemies of the people and other scum.'

-ЧТОБЫ ЧЕРЕЗ ЧАС ПРИЗНАНИЯ ЭТОГО ВРАГА БЫЛИ У МЕНЯ НА СТОЛЕ!...
-ТОВАРИЩ ОСОБОУПОЛНОМОЧЕННЫЙ, МЫ ЗА ЭТО ВРЕМЯ ЭТОМУ ГАДУ
ЯЙЦА ОТОРВЁМ И ЖАРЕНУЮ КОТЛЕТУ СДЕЛАЕМ ИЗ ЭТОГО ЖИДА...

'I give you one hour to put the confession* of this enemy [of the people] on my desk!'
'Don't you worry, Comrade Plenipotentiary. In an hour, we'll have torn his balls off and fried this yid like a steak.'

* 'When [Nikolai] Bukharin's first wife, Nadezhda Lukina was interrogated, her brother Mikhail was among the members of the family who were tortured to give evidence against the others and her. A recent Soviet article gives a horrifying account of his withdrawing his evidence and then, after further interrogation, confirming it again. The article quotes another former prisoner, a woman who, asking "How could a brother give evidence against a sister?" answered that a Comintern worker in her cell came back from interrogation one day, complaining bitterly that a close comrade had incriminated her; the examiners had shown her the testimony in his own handwriting. Soon afterward, she returned from a further session. This time she cried, "How could I? How could I? Today I had a confrontation with him and I saw not a man, but live raw meat."' Robert Conquest, *The Great Terror: A Reassessment*, 1990.

– МЫ ИЗ ТЕБЯ ВСЮ АНТИПАРТИЙНУЮ ПЫЛЬ ВЫТРЯХНЕМ, ЧТОБЫ НЕ КЛЕ-
ВЕТАЛ НА ВОЖДЕЙ КПСС, ЯКОБЫ ОНИ ВСЕ ЗВЕРИНАЯ СМЕСЬ ПОЛИТИ-
ЧЕСКИХ АВАНТЮРИСТОВ, БАНДЫ УБИЙЦ И ДИКИХ ЭКСПЛУАТАТОРОВ...

'We'll whack all the anti-Party dust out of you.* You won't go slandering and spreading lies about the leaders of the Communist Party – calling them a bestial mixture of political adventurers, a gang of murderers and savage exploiters.'

* The interrogators have wrapped the prisoner in a carpet so no signs of torture will show on the body. This precaution was taken in the event that the subject might later appear in a public trial.

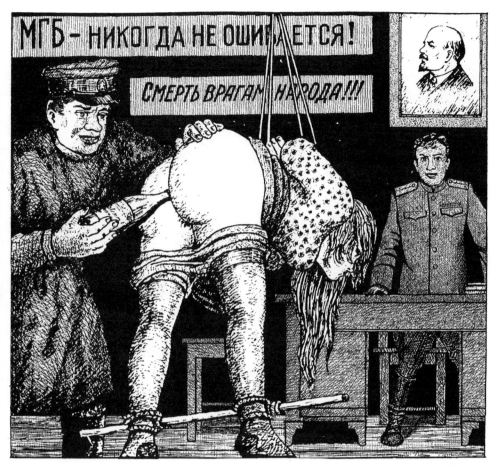

– НУ, КУРВА, СЕЙЧАС МЫ ТЕБЯ УГОСТИМ НАШИМ СОВЕТСКИМ ШАМПАНСКИМ, ВОТ ТОГДА РАЗВЯЖЕШЬ СВОЙ ВРАЖИЙ ЯЗЫК...

The placards on the wall read (from top to bottom): **'MGB Never Makes Mistakes!'**; **'Death to the Enemies of the People!!!'**.

'Well, bitch, now we're going to treat you to some Soviet Champagne.* It'll loosen your enemy tongue!'

* Soviet Champagne – *Sovetskoe Shampanskoe*, is the brand name of the official Soviet champagne, which was first created in 1928. Different methods of fermentation to traditional champagne allowed for mass-production. It was made available to every Soviet citizen in an attempt to show the world that they were able to enjoy the same luxury goods as their counterparts in capitalist countries.

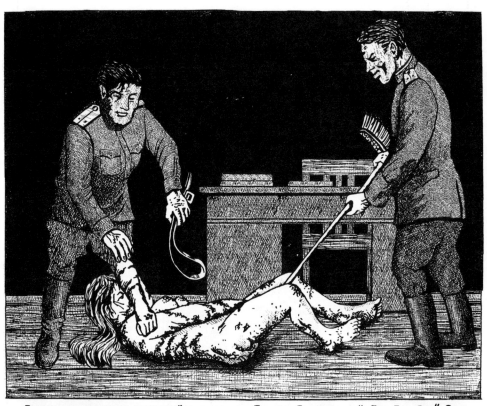

-ГОВОРИ, КТО ЕЩЕ С ТОБОЙ СЛУШАЛ „ГОЛОС АМЕРИКИ", „БИ-БИ-СИ", „СВО-
БОДУ" И РАСПРОСТРАНЯЛ АНТИСОВЕТСКУЮ ПРОПАГАНДУ ИЛИ Я ТЕБЕ
ЗАСУНУ РУЧКУ ШВАБРЫ В ТВОЮ ВОНЮЧУЮ ЩЕЛКУ И ОНА ВЫЙДЕТ...
ЧЕРЕЗ ТВОЙ ПОГАНЫЙ РОТ!...

'Tell us who else listened to the Voice of America, BBC, and Radio Freedom, and distributed anti-Soviet propaganda with you, or I'll stick this broom all the way up your stinking arse until it comes right out of your filthy mouth!'

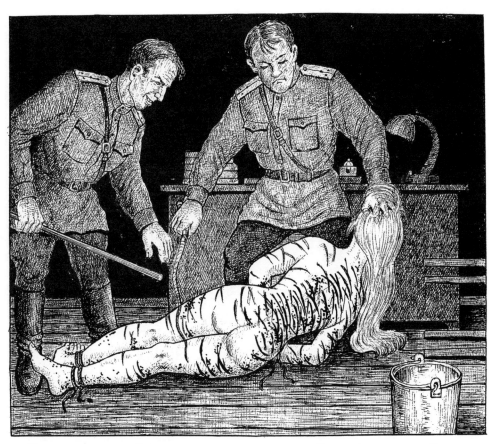

— ГОВОРИ, СУКА! КАКИЕ РАЗГОВОРЫ ВЁЛ ДОМА ТВОЙ МУЖ
ПРОТИВ СОВЕТСКОЙ ВЛАСТИ И ПАРТИИ КОММУНИСТОВ?...

'Talk, bitch! What was your husband saying at home against the Soviet authorities and the Communist Party?'

–ПРИЗНАВАЙСЯ! ТЫ ПРОНИК В РЯДЫ ВКП(б), СТАВ СЕКРЕТА-РЁМ ГОРКОМА И ОБКОМА, ВРЕДИЛ НАШЕЙ ПАРТИИ ИЗНУТРИ!...

'Confess! You have penetrated the ranks of the VKP(b), become secretary of the municipal committee and wrecked our Party from the inside!'*

* The prospect of arrest and trial weighed heavy even on the highest-ranking Party member. Following their arrest, aware of the fate that awaited them, many immediately asked to sign their 'confession'. Others, unable to comprehend what was happening, remained loyal to the Party, believing that it would eventually realise its mistake and reinstate them. 'They were all tired men. The higher you got in the hierarchy, the more tired they were. I have nowhere seen such exhausted men as among the higher strata of Soviet politicians, among the Old Bolshevik guard. It was not only the effect of overwork, nervous strain and apprehension. It was the past that was telling on them, the years of conspiracy, prison and exile; the years of the famine and the Civil War; and sticking to the rules of a game that demanded that at every moment a man's whole life should be at stake. They were indeed 'dead men on furlough', as Lenin had called them. Nothing could frighten them any more, nothing surprise them. They had given all they had. History had squeezed them out to the last drop, had burnt them out to the last spiritual calorie; yet they were still glowing in cold devotion, like phosphorescent corpses.' Arthur Koestler, *Arrow in the Blue*, 1945, (quoted by: Robert Conquest, *The Great Terror: A Reassessment*, 1990).

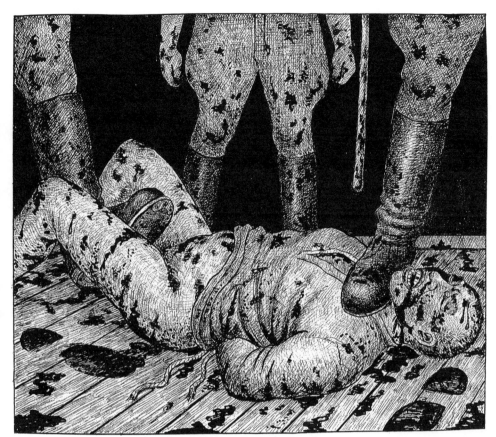

−Я... АНГЛИЙСКИЙ, ФРАНЦУЗСКИЙ, АМЕРИКАНСКИЙ, ЯПОН-
СКИЙ, ИТАЛЬЯНСКИЙ, НЕМЕЦКИЙ И ЕЩЁ КАКОЙ-ТО ШПИОН...

'I am a British, French, American, Japanese, Italian, German and whatever else spy…'*

* 'Because falling under suspicion was in itself considered a sign of guilt, prisoners were rarely released without serving at least a partial sentence. Lev Finklestein, a Russian Jew arrested in the late 1940s, had the impression that although no one had managed to invent a particularly plausible case against him, he had been given a short camp sentence simply in order to prove that the arresting organs never made a mistake. Another ex-prisoner, S. G. Durasova, even claims that she was specifically told, by one of her investigators, that "we never arrest anyone who is not guilty. And even if you weren't guilty, we can't release you, because then people would say that we are picking up innocent people."' Anne Applebaum, *Gulag: A History*, 2003.

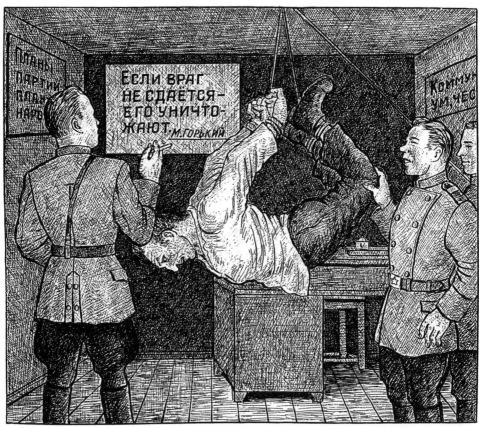

— ТАК ЭТОМУ ЕВРЕЙСКОМУ СИОНИСТУ БУДЕТ ЛЕГЧЕ ВС-
ПОМНИТЬ О ЧЛЕНСТВЕ В МИРОВОМ ЖИДО-МАСОНСКОМ
ЗАГОВОРЕ...

Text on the left wall reads: **'The plans of the Party are the plans of the people'**; text on the back wall reads: **'If the enemy doesn't surrender – destroy him. Maxim Gorky'**; text on the right wall (partially visible) reads: **'Communism is the mind, honour, and conscience of our time'.**

'This'll make it easier for this Jewish Zionist to recall his membership in the Judeo-Masonic conspiracy.'*

* The authorities believed in the existence of a coalition between Jews and Freemasons to gain world domination, regularly blaming the Judeo-Masonic conspiracy theory for the shortcomings of their own system. Throughout the book Baldaev reflects this paranoia by giving exaggerated Jewish characteristics to some of his protagonists.

Наказание зэка за нападение на прокурора по надзору за УМЗ — смирительной рубашкой

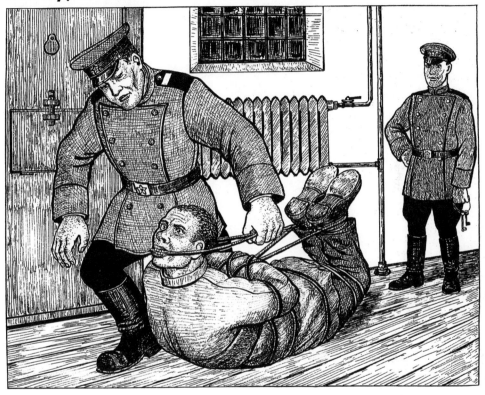

При тугом пеленании в смирительную рубашку „с уздечкой" зэк выдерживает не более 30-35 минут и просит прощения за свой дерзкий поступок...

A straight jacket put on a convict for assault of the prosecutor supervising the UMZ.*

When a straight jacket with a 'bridle'† was tightened on a convict, he could bear no more than thirty to thirty-five minutes before he would repent his brazen acts.

* UMZ (*Upravlenie Mest Zaklyucheniya*) – the Directorate of Imprisonment Facilities

† 'Let us try to list some of the simplest methods which break the will and the character of the prisoner... bridling (also known as "the swan dive")? This was a Sukhanovka method – also used in Archangel, where the interrogator Ivkov applied it in 1940. A long piece of rough towelling was inserted between the prisoner's jaws like a bridle; the ends were then pulled back over his shoulders and tied to his heels. Just try lying on your stomach like a wheel, with your spine breaking – and without water and food for two days!' Aleksandr Solzhenitsyn, *The Gulag Archipelago*, 1973.

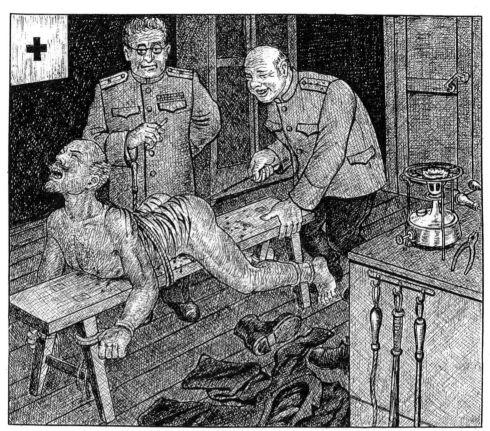

**–КАК ПРОЧИСТИМ ЕМУ ОЧКО, БЫСТРО ВСПОМНИТ, КАК ВРЕД-
ИЛ СОВЕТСКОЙ ВЛАСТИ И ПАРТИИ В НАУЧНО-ИССЛЕДОВА-
ТЕЛЬСКОМ ИНСТИТУТЕ СВОЕЙ КИБЕРНЕТИКОЙ...**

'Once we've cleaned up his arse, he'll quickly remember how he damaged Soviet power and the Party with that cybernetics* of his in his research institute…'

* During the 1950s the fledgling Western science of cybernetics (the comparative study of regulatory mechanisms, which enabled the construction of the first computers), was mocked by the Soviet propaganda machine as an attempt to replace human beings with robots. At the same time as Russian scientists were secretly developing their own computers using cybernetic systems, publicly the Western scientific ideology on which they were basing their work was dismissed as 'utterly hostile to people and science', (Mikhail Iaroshevsky, *Literaturnaia Gazeta*, 1952). Many scientists were arrested for working in this officially forbidden area and it was not until the 1960s that its status as a 'weapon of imperialist ideology' was politically revised.

ОДИН ИЗ ЗВЕРСКИХ ПРИЁМОВ ВЫРВАТЬ ПРИЗНАНИЕ У „ВРАГА НАРОДА"-„ПЕРЕКРЫТЬ КИСЛОРОД ИЛИ ПИЩИК..."

ВО ВРЕМЯ ДОПРОСА СПЕЦИАЛЬНЫЕ РАБОТНИКИ НКВД „МОЛОТО-БОЙЦЫ ИЛИ КОЛУНЫ," В ПОМОЩЬ СЛЕДОВАТЕЛЯМ (ЧАСТО И САМИ СЛЕДОВАТЕЛИ) ОДЕВАЛИ НА ГОЛОВУ ЖЕРТВЕ РЕЗИНОВЫЙ МЕ-ШОК ДЛЯ ПЕРЕКРЫТИЯ ДЫХАНИЯ. ПОСЛЕ НЕСКОЛЬКИХ ТАКИХ ПРИЁМОВ У ЖЕРТВЫ ШЛА КРОВЬ ИЗ НОСА, РТА, УШЕЙ...

An example of an atrocious method of extracting confessions from an 'enemy of the people': 'cutting off the oxygen', or 'squeezing the reed'.

During interrogations, a special NKVD brigade (or, sometimes, the interrogators themselves), known as 'hammerers' or 'splitting axes', put a rubber bag over the head of the victim to temporarily suffocate him. After this technique had been used a few times, the victim would start bleeding from the nose, ears and mouth.

-ТЫ, ГАД, БЫВШИЙ КОЛХОЗНЫЙ БРИГАДИР, С ВРЕДИТЕЛЬСКОЙ ЦЕЛЬЮ ПОДСАЛИВАЛ КОРОВАМ СЕНО! СОЗНАЙСЯ, ЧТО ТЫ ВРАГ!...

'You bastard, former kolkhoz foreman, you wrecked the cows' hay by mixing it with salt. Confess that you are an enemy!'

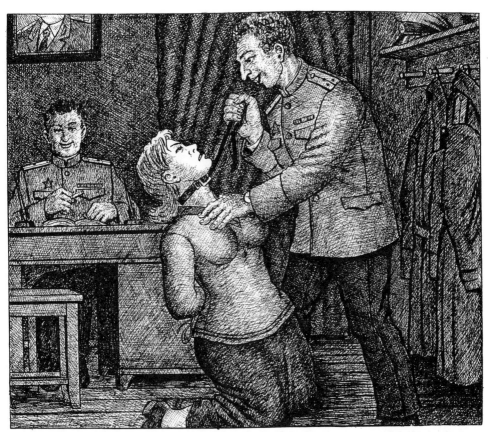

—ГОВОРИ, УЧЕНАЯ ТВАРЬ, КАК ПРОПОВЕДОВАЛА БУРЖУАЗНУЮ
АНТИСОВЕТСКУЮ ЛЖЕНАУКУ ГЕНЕТИКУ НА КАФЕДРЕ, ИЛИ
СЕЙЧАС БУДЕШЬ ДЫШАТЬ ЧЕРЕЗ ЗАДНЮЮ ДЫРКУ...

'Tell me now, you educated animal, about how you preached genetics,* that bourgeois anti-Soviet ersatz science, in your university department, or you'll be breathing through your arsehole!'

* Communism rejected theories of hereditary genetics, preferring to follow its officially sanctioned scientist Trofim Lysenko. He adopted the theory of inheritance of acquired characteristics (perceived as a socialist model in the field of science) over Darwinism, and was championed by Stalin. Scientific dissent of his work was outlawed in 1948, and many of those who questioned it were imprisoned. His experiments on methods of increasing agricultural production failed to yield results, and he falsified many of his findings. Following Stalin's death in 1953 his influence waned and his work was officially discredited in 1964.

В ГОДЫ КУЛЬТА АРЕСТОВАННЫХ ДОМА, НА РАБОТЕ „ВРАГОВ НАРОДА" ПРИ ДОСТАВКЕ В ТЮРЬМУ САЖАЛИ В „ОТСТОЙНИК"...

В ТЮРЕМНЫЕ „ОТСТОЙНИКИ" НА 10 м² ВТАЛКИВАЛОСЬ ПО 45-50 ЧЕЛОВЕК НА 1-3 СУТОК БЕЗ ВОДЫ И ПИЩИ ДЛЯ „ДУХОВНОГО СЛОМА". ОТ ТЕСНОТЫ И ДУХОТЫ НЕКОТОРЫЕ УМИРАЛИ, И ИХ ТРУПЫ СТОЯЛИ В ПЛОТНОЙ ЛЮДСКОЙ МАССЕ. В ТУАЛЕТ „ВРАГОВ НАРОДА" НЕ ПУСКАЛИ, И ОНИ ВЫНУЖДЕНЫ БЫЛИ СПРАВЛЯТЬ ЕСТЕСТВЕННЫЕ НАДОБНОСТИ В ШТАНЫ. СТЕНЫ „ОТСТОЙНИКА" ПОКРЫВАЛИСЬ ВОНЮЧЕЙ СЛИЗЬЮ...

During the reign of the cult of personality, the 'enemies of the people' arrested at home or at work were put into 'settling tanks'.

Forty-five to fifty people were crammed into the prison 'settling tanks', with an area of ten square meters.* They were left there without food or water for between one and three days for 'spiritual breakdown'. Without enough room or fresh air to breathe some died, their corpses stood upright, squeezed in between other people's bodies. The 'enemies of the people' were not allowed to use the toilet, and they had no choice but to relieve themselves without taking their clothes off. The walls of the 'settling tank' were covered in foul-smelling slime.

* 'She told me that it sometimes happens in those crowded prisons that one of the prisoners will have a fit of hysteria and begin to scream, which spreads to others until perhaps hundreds are screaming uncontrollably. [She] says people who live near the OGPU place in Moscow have heard the screaming more than once and describe it as terrifying.' Reader Bullard, *Inside Stalin's Russia: The Diaries of Reader Bullard 1930-1934*, 2000, (edited by Julian and Margaret Bullard).

ОДНО ИЗ ОТДЕЛЕНИЙ ЛЮДСКОГО УБОЙНОГО ЦЕХА НКВД-МГБ КОНЦА 40-Х ГОДОВ (ВТОРАЯ КРОВАВАЯ ВОЛНА СТАЛИНСКОГО ТЕРРОРА ПОСЛЕ 30-Х ГОДОВ). РАССТРЕЛ „ВРАГОВ НАРОДА", ЛИТЕЙНЫЙ ПР., Д. 4 (ПОДВАЛЬНОЕ ПОМЕЩЕНИЕ СО СТОРОНЫ УЛ. ВОИНОВА).

One of the departments of the human slaughterhouse of the NKVD-MVD, in the late 1940s (the second wave of Stalin's bloody purges after the 1930s). The execution of the 'enemies of the people' at 4 Liteiny Prospekt* in Leningrad, Russia (the basement on the side of Voinov Street).

* 4 Liteiny Prospekt was the address of the headquarters of the NKVD. Referred to colloquially as the 'Big House', it had an infamous reputation – few who entered ever left.

Journey to the Camp

В ГОДЫ КУЛЬТА СОВЕРШЕННО БЕЗВИННЫХ „ВРАГОВ НАРОДА" 10 МИЛЛИОНОВ ЭТАПИРОВАЛИ НА „КОЛЫМУ...

ЗАКЛЮЧЁННЫХ „ВРАГОВ НАРОДА", НЕ ВЫДЕРЖАВШИХ ПЕШИЕ ЭТАПЫ В СОТНИ И ТЫСЯЧИ КИЛОМЕТРОВ, КОНВОЙ ГУЛАГА НКВД РАССТРЕЛИВАЛ И ЗАКАЛЫВАЛ ШТЫКАМИ ФИЗИЧЕСКИ СЛАБЫХ, БОЛЬНЫХ, ПЫТАВШИХСЯ БЕЖАТЬ, ЗАХРОМАВШИХ, СОШЕДШИХ С УМА. КАЖДЫЙ ЭТАП СОПРОВОЖДАЛА ПОХОРОННАЯ КОМАНДА ИЗ ФИЗИЧЕСКИ КРЕПКИХ ЗЭКОВ НА ГУЖЕВОМ ТРАНСПОРТЕ С ШАНЦЕВЫМ ИНСТРУМЕНТОМ... ТРУПЫ ХОРОНИЛИ ГОЛЫМИ. ИЗ ТЫСЯЧИ ЗЭКОВ К МЕСТУ НАЗНАЧЕНИЯ ПРИБЫВАЛО 700-800 ЧЕЛ.

During the years of the cult of personality, ten million innocent 'enemies of the people' were transported to Kolyma.*

Convicts who could not endure deportation marches of hundreds, or even thousands of kilometres, were executed by the guards of the Gulag. The weak, sickly, or lame, and convicts who tried to escape or went insane, were shot or stabbed to death with bayonets. Each deportation group had its own burial brigade made up of physically fit convicts. They travelled on horse-driven carts and were equipped with shovels. The bodies were buried naked. Out of a thousand convicts, only seven to eight hundred would finally make it to the prison camp.

* The Kolyma region in Russia's Far East was home to a vast and notorious camp system, developed between 1932 and 1954. An area rich in natural resources, Gulag labour was used for gold mining and lumbering, as well as road building and construction. It is estimated half a million prisoners died there in the shocking camp conditions and harsh climate (winter temperatures regularly reach -70° C).

ПРОДАЖА КОНВОЕМ „ЖИВОГО ТОВАРА" УГОЛОВНИКАМ НА ЭТАПЕ...
ОСОБО ЦЕНИЛИСЬ ДЕВУШКИ И ЖЕНЩИНЫ ИЗ ПРИБАЛТИКИ: ЛА-
ТЫШКИ, ЛИТОВКИ, НЕМКИ, ПОЛЬКИ И ЭСТОНКИ, КОТОРЫХ НАСИ-
ЛОВАЛИ ГРУППОЙ. НЕКОТОРЫЕ АВТОРИТЕТНЫЕ „ВОРЫ В ЗАКОНЕ"
ИМЕЛИ В СВОЕЙ „СОБСТВЕННОСТИ" 2-3 ТАКИХ ЗЭЧКИ ИЗ „КОНТРЫ"...

Guards selling 'livestock' to convicts during penal transportation.[*]
Women from the Baltic regions – Latvia, Lithuania, Estonia, as well as Germany and Poland – had the highest value. They were gang-raped by the convicts. Some authoritative 'legitimate' thieves[†] 'owned' two or three women 'contra' (counter-revolutionary) prisoners.

[*] 'Penal transportation' was the process of deporting criminals to a penal institution.
[†] The *vory v zakone* (thieves in law) are 'legitimate' thieves who belong to a criminal organisation similar in structure to the mafia. In the Gulag the authorities generally granted them the status of trustees, giving them complete dominance over those perceived to be ideologically unsound: political and religious prisoners. They exerted a great influence, acting like a shadow administration. Following their own strict 'thieves' code', they meted out severe punishments to those within their ranks who broke it. They spoke their own argot and their bodies were covered by a complex system of tattoos, only understood by the initiated, which were used to display the wearer's position within their hierarchy (see: Danzig Baldaev, *Russian Criminal Tattoo Encyclopaedia Volume I, II, III*, 2003-2008).

В ГОДЫ СТАЛИНИЗМА КОММУНИСТАМИ БЫЛИ ДЕПОРТИРОВАНЫ В ВОСТОЧНЫЕ И СЕВЕРНЫ
ЛАТЫШИ, ЧЕЧЕНЫ, ИНГУШИ, БАЛКАРЦЫ, КАРАЧАЕВЦЫ, КАЛМЫКИ, ГРЕКИ, ТУРКИ, КРЫМСКИЕ,
(ИЗ-ЗА ГИБЕЛИ ОТ НЕЧЕЛОВЕЧЕСКИХ РАБСКИХ УСЛОВИЙ). КРОМЕ НЕМЦЕВ И КРЫМСКИХ Т

The 'traitor peoples' before they were sent to slavery in Stalin's Socialist Gulag.

During the Stalin era, Communists deported around two million ethnically non-Russian people to the eastern and northern parts of the USSR: Finns, Germans, Poles, Estonians, Lithuanians, Latvians, Chechens, Ingush, Balkarians, Karachaevs, Kalmyks, Greeks, Turks, Crimea Tartars, Western Ukrainians. After the rehabilitation,

...Ы ОКОЛО 2 МЛН. НЕРУССКОГО НАСЕЛЕНИЯ: ФИННЫ, НЕМЦЫ, ПОЛЯКИ, ЭСТОНЦЫ, ЛИТОВЦЫ, ...Е УКРАИНЦЫ, ПОЛОВИНА КОТОРЫХ ПОСЛЕ РЕАБИЛИТАЦИИ НЕ ВЕРНУЛИСЬ НА СВОИ ЗЕМЛИ ...ИТИРОВАНЫ, НО НАКАЗАНИЕ ПРОДОЛЖАЕТСЯ – КПСС НЕ ПУСКАЕТ ИХ НА ПРЕЖНИЕ ЗЕМЛИ...

half of them never returned home, perishing in the harsh and inhumane conditions. With the exception of Germans and Crimean Tartars, all have been rehabilitated, but the punishment continues – the Communist Party does not allow them to return home.[*]

[*] Baldaev was writing before the fall of Communism.

Будни ГУЛАГА МВД

Коммунисты-бюрократы убийцы: демократии, десятков миллионов людей, природы и всего жи

ПОГРУЗКА В СЕТКАХ ОЧЕРЕДНОГО ЭТАПА РАБОВ ГУЛАГА НА „КУРОРТНЫЙ" ПАРО КРАЯ Г. МАГАДАН. ВПОСЛЕДСТВИИ СЕТКИ ИЗ-ЗА БОЛЬШОГО ТРАВМАТИЗМ

Text on the left reads: '**Daily Life of the MVD Gulag. Communists are murderous bureaucrats. They eradicated democracy, tens of millions of people, nature, and everything alive...**'; verse on the right reads: '**I remember that port in Vanino / And the grim-looking steamboat. / We boarded, walking up the gangway, / Up into cold, gruesome prisons.***[ ]**'.

The loading of Gulag slaves in fishing nets onto the *Yalta* 'pleasure boat' in the Vanino port. The boat was bound for the seaport in Magadan, the capital of the Kolyma prison camp region. Later, due to the high rate of injury, the nets were replaced with metal cages, with a capacity of fifty to sixty people each.[†]

Я ПОМНЮ ТОТ ВАНИНСКИЙ ПОРТ
И ВИД ПАРОХОДА УГРЮМЫЙ,
КАК ШЛИ МЫ ПО ТРАПУ НА БОРТ
В ХОЛОДНЫЕ МРАЧНЫЕ ТРЮМЫ...

ПОРТУ ВАНИНО ДЛЯ ДОСТАВКИ В ПОРТ СТОЛИЦЫ КАТОРЖНОГО КОЛЫМСКОГО
МЕТАЛЛИЧЕСКИМИ КЛЕТКАМИ ВМЕСТИМОСТЬЮ НА 50-60 ЧЕЛОВЕК.

* The verse is from a well-known prisoner song, popular in the USSR. Often called 'The Anthem of Kolyma Prisoners', it was written around 1946 (exact date and author unknown).
† 'In that immense, cavernous, murky hold were crammed more than two thousand women. From the floor to the ceiling, as in a gigantic poultry farm, they were cooped up in open cages, five of them in each nine-feet-square space. The floor was covered with more women. Because of the heat and humidity, most of them were only scantily dressed; some had even stripped down to nothing. The lack of washing facilities and the relentless heat had covered their bodies with ugly red spots, boils and blisters. The majority were suffering from some form of skin disease or other, apart from stomach ailments and dysentery.' Michael Solomon, *Magadan*, 1971.

1937-53гг. МАССОВОЕ ИЗНАСИЛОВАНИЕ ЖЕНЩИН-"ВРАГОВ НАРОДА
УГОЛОВНИКАМИ. НАСИЛОВАЛИ СТАРЫХ И МОЛОДЫХ. КТО СОПРОТИВ/
ЖИВОТ И ДР. ЧАСТИ ТЕЛА.... МАССОВЫЕ ИЗНАСИЛОВАНИЯ БЫЛИ Н/
МЫ, ПРОБИВ ОТСЕЧНУЮ СТЕНКУ, ПРИ ПОПУСТИТЕЛЬСТВЕ КОНВОЯ И

1937–1953. Mass rape of women, 'enemies of the people', by criminal prisoners on the *Tobol* steamboat during the Vanino Port – Nagaevo Bay – Magadan deportation. Both young and old women were raped. Those who tried to resist were stabbed to death or strangled. Many were stabbed with knives in the vagina, stomach, and other parts of the body. Mass rapes took place on the *Minsk*, *Yalta*, and other cargo ships. The convicts entered the holds, breaking through the partition walls, with the collusion of the guards and crew.[*]

ЭДЕ „ТОБОЛ" ПРИ ЭТАПЕ (ПОРТ ВАНИНО-БУХТА НАГАЕВО-г. МАГАДАН)
I ЗАРЕЗАНЫ,ЗАДУШЕНЫ,МНОГИМ ВТЫКАЛИ НОЖИ ВО ВЛАГАЛИЩЕ,
IX „МИНСК",„ЯЛТА"И ДР.ПАРОХОДАХ.УГОЛОВНИКИ ПРОНИКАЛИ В ТРЮ-
ОМАНДЫ...

* 'Through the sharp torn edges of the wall, half-naked male criminals poured in, their tattooed bodies glistening with sweat. With frightening squeals and howls of the sort that medieval hordes must have emitted when attacking a particularly dangerous enemy, the men grabbed the nearest women and dragged them onto the bunks. The overcrowded hold was again filled with the women's plaintive screams and entreaties, which blended with the men's ululations and whoops... And we witnessed the opening scenes of endless gang rapes, known among the convicts as the "Kolyma Tram"... Women who resisted were killed on the spot. Many of the convicts were armed with knives, razors, and spikes and here and there fights flared up among them. From time to time, to the accompaniment of foul obscenities and cheers, they tossed down corpses from the upper bunks – the women they had tortured to death.' Elena Glinka, The Big Kolyma Tram, *Russian Life*, 1988.

The Gulag System

ОТДЕЛЬНЫЙ ЛАГЕРНЫЙ ПУНКТ (
ОЛП — „ГЕНИАЛЬНОЕ" ИЗОБРЕТ

1. ЗДАНИЕ АДМИНИСТРАЦИИ
2. УЧ. КЛАССЫ ВВ И СТОЛОВАЯ
3. ОТДЕЛЕНИЕ ДЛЯ ИНВАЛИДОВ
4. ШТРАФНОЙ ИЗОЛЯТОР
5. МОРГ
6. БОЛЬНИЦА И КУХНЯ
7. АПТЕКА, ПОЧТА, ЦЕНЗУРА
8. ЛАРЁК
9. ПРОЕЗД-ПРОХОД В ЗОНУ, ЧАСТЬ
10. КПП, ШЛЮЗ, ЦЕНТР. ВОРОТА
11. СКЛАД ГСМ
12. ЭЛЕКТРОПОДСТАНЦИЯ
13. ЗДАНИЕ ДЛЯ СПЕЦИАЛИСТОВ
14. ПРОМЫШЛЕННАЯ ЗОНА
15. ПЛАЦ ДЛЯ ЗЭКОВ
16. УБОРНАЯ
17. БАРАК ДЛЯ РАБОТНИКОВ ОЛП-ИТЛ
18. ОФИЦЕРСКИЙ БАРАК
19. КАЗАРМА ДЛЯ СОЛДАТ ВВ МВД
20. ГАРАЖ ОХРАНЫ МВД
21. ПИТОМНИК СЛУЖЕБНЫХ СОБАК
22. ЖИЛАЯ ЗОНА ДЛЯ ЗЭКОВ
23. ВНУТРЕННИЕ КПП
24. БИБЛИОТЕКА
25. СЕКЦИЯ ОБЩ. ПОРЯДКА
26. СТОРОЖЕВАЯ ВЫШКА ВВ МВД
27. ЛЕДНИК
28. ОВОЩНОЙ СКЛАД
29. ПРОДУКТОВЫЙ СКЛАД
30. СТОЛОВАЯ ДЛЯ ЗЭКОВ
31. КЛУБ
32. СПОРТПЛОЩАДКА
33. ПОРТНОВСКАЯ И САПОЖНАЯ
34. ВОДОКАЧКА
35. КОТЕЛЬНАЯ И ПРАЧЕЧНАЯ
36. КУЗНИЦА И СЛЕСАРНАЯ
37. ГАРАЖ
38. СТОЛЯРНАЯ
39. ВЕЩЕВОЙ СКЛАД
40. БАНЯ
41. ТЕПЛИЦА
42. ПОЖАРНАЯ ЧАСТЬ
43. КОНЮШНЯ И ХОЗДВОР
44. СВИНАРНИК
45. СТРЕЛЬБИЩЕ
46. КЛАДБИЩЕ ДЛЯ ЗЭКОВ

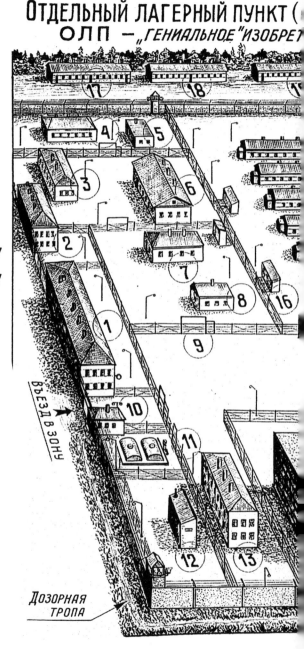

ВЪЕЗД В ЗОНУ

ДОЗОРНАЯ ТРОПА

ГА НКВД-МВД ДЛЯ СОДЕРЖАНИЯ 1,5-2 ТЫСЯЧИ ЗЭКОВ
"УНИСТОВ ПО УМЕРЩВЛЕНИЮ РАБСКИМ ТРУДОМ "КЛАССОВЫХ ВРАГОВ"

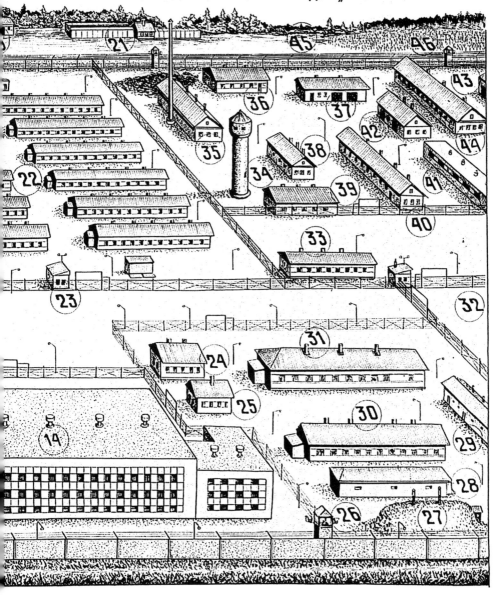

63

A Separate Camp Point (OLP)* of the Gulag of the NKVD-MVD for 1,500–2,000 prisoners.
The OLP was an 'ingenious' invention of the Communists for killing 'class enemies' through slave labour.

Top left arrow: Entrance to the camp

Bottom left corner arrow: Watch path

1. Administration building
2. Classes for internal troops and canteen
3. Building for the disabled
4. Isolation cells
5. Morgue
6. Hospital and kitchen
7. Drugstore, post, and censorship quarters
8. Vendor stand
9. Entranceway to the camp
10. Checkpoint, central gates
11. Fuel warehouse
12. Power plant
13. Specialists building
14. Industrial zone
15. Drill ground
16. Toilet
17. Barracks for OLP-ITL[†] employees
18. Officers' barracks
19. Internal troops quarters
20. MVD guards' garage
21. Kennels for guard dogs
22. Prisoners' barracks
23. Internal checkpoints

24. Library
25. Internal order section
26. Watchtower
27. Icebox
28. Vegetable warehouse
29. Foodstuffs warehouse
30. Canteen for prisoners
31. Club
32. Sports grounds
33. Tailor and shoemaker
34. Water pumping station
35. Boilerhouse and laundry
36. Smithery and metal workshop
37. Garage
38. Wood workshop
39. Clothing warehouse
40. Sauna
41. Greenhouse
42. Fire station
43. Stables and service facilities
44. Pigpen
45. Shooting grounds
46. Prisoners' graveyard

* OLP (*Otdelney Lagpunkt*) – Separate Labour Camp.
† ITL (*Ispravitelno-Trudovoy Lager*) – Corrective Labour Camp.

Схема

РАСПОЛОЖЕНИЯ РЕГИОНОВ (ЗОН) *ГУЛАГА СОЗДАННОГО 10 июня 1934г.* ПО УКАЗАНИЮ ПОЛИТБЮРО ЦК ВКП(б) И В РЕЗУЛЬТАТЕ ПУТЕМ ТЕРРОРА, ГЕНОЦИДА И АПАРТЕИДА БЫЛИ УМЕРЩВЛЕНЫ МИЛЛИОНЫ ГРАЖДАН ВО ИМЯ СВЕТЛОГО БУДУЩЕГО-КОММУНИЗМА

Особенности ГУЛАГА НКВД-МВД:

1. ГЛАВНАЯ ОСОБЕННОСТЬ В ТОМ, ЧТО НАЧАЛЬНИК ПОЛИТОТДЕЛА ГУЛАГА НЕПОСРЕДСТВЕННО ПОДЧИНЕН ОРГОТДЕЛУ ЦК ВКП(б)-КПСС И ФОРМАЛЬНО НАЧАЛЬНИКУ ГУЛАГА. ЦК ВКП(б)-КПСС ЯВЛЯЕТСЯ НЕПОСРЕДСТВЕННЫМ ИДЕЙНЫМ ВДОХНОВИТЕЛЕМ ВСЕЙ СИСТЕМЫ КОНЦЛАГЕРЕЙ И РАБСКОГО ТРУДА- КУЛАКОВ "И „ВРАГОВ НАРОДА".
2. НКВД-МВД ЯВЛЯЕТСЯ ПОСЛУШНЫМ ОРУДИЕМ ЦК ВКП(б)-КПСС.

Регионы ГУЛАГА:

I – „СЕВЗАПЛАГ"
II – „ЗАПЛАГ"
III – „ЮЖЗАПЛАГ"
IV – „УРАЛЛАГ"
V – „СЕВСИБЛАГ"
VI – „СИБЛАГ"
VII – „ЮЖЛАГ"
VIII – „ДАЛЬСТРОЙ"
IX – „ПРИМОРЛАГ"

★ ☠ ☭

Killing is no murder!

ВСЯ СИСТЕМА ГУЛАГА ИМЕЛА ДВЕ ЦЕЛИ:

1. КАРАТЕЛЬНОЙ ПОЛИТИКОЙ ПРИВЕСТИ К УНИЧТОЖЕНИЮ БОЛЬШЕЙ ЧАСТИ ЗЭКОВ.
2. ЛЮБЫМИ СРЕДСТВАМИ ВЫПОЛНИТЬ ТРУДПЛАНЫ ПРАВИТЕЛЬСТВА.

PLAN

Map of the regions (zones) of the Gulag, created on 10th June, 1934 by a decree of the Political Bureau of the Central Committee of the All-Union Communist Party of Bolsheviks. Millions of people died through purges, genocide and apartheid, in the name of the bright future.

The Italian text reads: 'The end justifies the means!'.

Distinctive features of the Gulag of NKVD-MVD:

1. The main distinctive feature was that the Head of the Political Department of the Gulag answered directly to the Organisation Department of the TsK* VKP(b) of the Communist Party. Nominally, he answered to the Chief Warden of the Gulag. The TsK VKP(b) was the sole ideologist of the entire system of prison camps and slave labour of the *kulaks* and the 'enemies of the people'.

2. The NKVD-MVD was the obedient weapon of the TsK VKP(b).

Gulag Regions:
i Sevzaplag (Northwest)
ii Zaplag (West)
iii Yuzhzaplag (Southwest)
iv Urallag (Urals)

Il fine giustifica i mezzi !

„ОТ НЕУСТАННОЙ ЗАБОТЫ КОММУНИСТОВ И ГУЛАГА СТРАНА ПРЕВРАТИЛАСЬ В ЭКОНОМИЧЕСКИ ТЯЖЕЛО БОЛЬНОЕ, БЕЗДУХОВНОЕ И АГРЕССИВНОЕ ГОСУДАРСТВО.* В. НЕКРАСОВ

v Sevsiblag (Northern Siberia)

vi Siblag (Siberia)

vii Yuzhlag (South)

viii Dalstroy (Far East)

ix Primorlag (Primorie)

The Gulag system pursued two goals:

1. To exterminate the majority of convicts through punitive policies.

2. To meet the labour quotas set by the government by any means necessary.

'The tireless efforts of the Communists and the Gulag turned the country into an economically ill, dispirited, and aggressive state.' Victor Nekrasov.[†]

* TsK (*Tsentralny Kommitet*) – the Central Committee (of the Communist Party).
[†] Victor Nekrasov (1911–1987), Russian writer, journalist and editor. An outspoken critic of Stalinism, he was expelled from the Communist Party in 1973 and emigrated to France in 1974.

The alphabetical list (far from complete) of the cities and settlements, near which were located ITL (Corrective Labour Camps), OLP (Separate Camp Points), sharashkas (secret R&D laboratories in the Gulag system), komandirovkas,* construction sites, service centres, columns, roads, OKB (Special Design Offices), ITK (Corrective Labour Camps / Colonies), and special settlements of the Gulag.

1. Abakan *(vi)
2. Abez-Inta *(i)
3. Aim (viii)
4. Akmolinsk *(vi)
5. Aktyubinsk *(vi)
6. Aleksandrovskoye (vi)
7. Aldan *(vi)
8. Allaykha (viii)
9. Alma-Ata (vii)
10. Andizhan *(v)
11. Arkhangelsk *(i)
12. Askold Isle (viii)
13. Astrakhan *(iii)
14. Asha (iv)
15. Ayan *(viii)
16. Baku *(iii)
17. Balychigan *(viii)
18. Belomorsk *(i)
19. Belushye (i)
20. Berezovo (v)
21. Birobidzhan (ix)
22. Bodaybo *(vi)
23. Borovichi (ii)
24. Byreya *(ix)
25. Byugyuke (v)
26. Vanz (i)
27. Vaygach Isle (i)
28. Velsk (i)
29. Vereshchagino (v)
30. Verkhoyansk *(viii)
31. Verkhne-Imbatskoye (v)
32. Verkhne-Uralsk (iv)
33. Verkhny Ufaley *(iv)
34. Veslyana (v)
35. Vilyuisk *(vi)
36. Vitim *(vi)
37. Vologda *(ii)
38. Volkhov (ii)
39. Vorkuta *(i)
40. Vytegra *(i)
41. Gorali (v)
42. Gorky *(ii)
43. Dzhezkazgan *(vii)
44. Dnepropetrovsk *(iii)
45. Elabuga (ii)
46. Erofey Pavlovich *(vi)
47. Zhigansk (v)
48. Zayarsk (v)
49. Franz Joseph Land *(i)
50. Zyryanka (viii)
51. Ivanovo (ii)
52. Ivdel *(iv)
53. Izhevsk *(ii)
54. Izvestkovy (viii)
55. Iman (viii)
56. Irgiz (vii)

57. Irkutsk *(vi)
58. Ishimbay *(iv)
59. Kagan (vii)
60. Kazalinsk (vii)
61. Kazan *(ii)
62. Kamchatka *(viii)
63. Kandalaksha *(i)
64. Karabash (iv)
65. Karaganda *(vi)
66. Karakas (vii)
67. Karaul (v)
68. Kargopol *(i)
69. Kashin (ii)
70. Kemerovo *(vi)
71. Kzyl-Orda (vii)
72. Kizel *(ii)
73. Kirov (Vyatka) *(ii)
74. Knyazh-Pogost (i)
75. Kozhva (i)
76. Kokchetav *(vi)
77. Kolbashevo (vi)
78. Kolyma *(viii)
79. Commander Islands *(viii)
80. Komsomolsk *(ix)
81. Kondopoga *(i)
82. Kopeisk *(iv)
83. Kostroma *(ii)
84. Kotlas *(i)
85. Krasnovodsk (iv)
86. Krasnoturinsk (iv)
87. Krasnogorsk *(vi)
88. Kuznetsk *(vi)
89. Kuibyshev *(ii)
90. Kuloy (i)
91. Kungur *(iv)
92. Kurgan-Tyube *(vii)
93. Kuril Islands *(viii)
94. Kurya (i)
95. Kustanay *(vi)
96. Kyzyl (vi)
97. Kyusyur (v)
98. Leningrad *(ii)
99. Leninogorsk (vi)
100. Magdagachi (viii)
101. Magnitogorsk *(iv)
102. Mariinsk *(vi)
103. Mayor-Krest (viii)
104. Makhachkala (iii)
105. Medvezhiegorsk (i)
106. Mezen (ii)
107. Miass *(iv)
108. Mirnoye (v)
109. Molotov (Perm) *(iv)
110. Molotovsk (i)
111. Monchegorsk (i)
112. Morshansk (ii)

113. Moscow *(ii)
114. Nalchik (iii)
115. Narian-Mar *(i)
116. Nikolayevsk (vi)
117. Nikopol (iii)
118. Nizhniye Kresty *(viii)
119. Nizhne-Tambovsk (viii)
120. Nizhny Tagil *(iv)
121. Novaya Zemlya *(i)
122. Nizhneye Shadrino (vi)
123. Novosibirsk *(vi)
124. Nordvik (v)
125. Norilsk *(v)
126. Ozhogino (viii)
127. Olyokminsk *(vi)
128. Omsk *(vi)
129. Orsk *(iv)
130. Ostashkov (ii)
131. Pakhta-Aral (vii)
132. Penza (ii)
133. Petrozavodsk *(i)
134. Petropavlovsk (vi)
135. Pechora *(i)
136. Plesetsk (i)
137. Podkamennaya Tunguska *(v)
138. Pokur (v)
139. Pokcha (i)
140. Prokopyevsk (vi)
141. Ramenskoye (ii)
142. Revda (iv)
143. Rezh (iv)
144. Rugoozero (i)
145. Savinobor (i)
146. Salekhard *(v)
147. Salyany (iii)
148. Sama (iv)
149. Saransk-Potma *(ii)
150. Sakhalin *(ix)
151. Sverdlovsk *(iv)
152. Svirstroy (ii)
153. Segezha (i)
154. Seychman *(viii)
155. Semipalatinsk *(vi)
156. Solikamsk *(iv)
157. Solovets Islands *(i)
158. Sortavala (i)
159. Srednekolymsk *(viii)
160. Sretinsk (vi)
161. Stalingrad *(iii)
162. Stalino (Donetsk) *(iii)
163. Stalinogorsk (ii)
164. Stalinsk (vi)
165. Stanchik (viii)
166. Starodub (ii)
167. Stolbovoye (viii)
168. Suojärvi *(i)

169. Sukhumi (iii)
170. Suchan *(ix)
171. Syzran *(ii)
172. Syktyvkar *(i)
173. Tavda *(iv)
174. Tayshet-Bratsk *(vi)
175. Tashkent *(vii)
176. Tbilisi (iii)
177. Tekyulyak (viii)
178. Tetyushi (ii)
179. Tiksi (v)
180. Tikhvin (ii)
181. Tobolsk *(vi)
182. Totma *(i)
183. Tomsk *(vi)
184. Tula (ii)
185. Tura (v)
186. Turinsk *(iv)
187. Turkestan *(vii)
188. Turukhansk *(v)
189. Tyumen *(vi)
190. Uglich (ii)
191. Ulyanovsk (ii)
192. Ulan-Ude *(vi)
193. Uman (iii)
194. Uralsk (iv)
195. Ust-Vorkuta *(i)
196. Ust-Vym *(i)
197. Ust-Kamenogorsk *(vi)
198. Ust-Kamchatsky *(viii)
199. Ust-Kulom *(i)
200. Ust-Mil *(iii)
201. Ust-Port (v)
202. Ust-Srednikan (viii)
203. Ust-Usa *(viii)
204. Ust-Ukhta *(i)
205. Ust-Shugor (i)
206. Ufa *(iv)
207. Fergana (vii)
208. Frunze (vii)
209. Khabarovsk *(ix)
210. Kholmogory (i)
211. Khonu (vii)
212. Chardzhou (vii)
213. Chelkar (vii)
214. Chelyabinsk *(iv)
215. Chita *(vi)
216. Chkalov (Orenburg) (iv)
217. Chusovoy *(iv)
218. Shadrinsk *(iv)
219. Shcherbakov (ii)
220. Ekibastuz-Ugol (vii)
221. Yakutsk *(v)
222. Yaroslavl (ii)

Алфавитный (далеко не полный) перечень городов и населенных пунктов, в районе которых располагались ИТЛ (исправительно-трудовые лагеря), ОЛП (отдельные лагпункты), лагучастки - "шарашки", командировки, стройобъекты, комбинаты, колонны, трассы, ОКБ (особые конструкторские бюро), ИТК (исправительно-трудовые колонии), спецпоселения ГУЛАГа НКВД-МВД:

#	Населённый пункт	Регион
1	АБАКАН •	VI
2	АБЕЗЬ-ИНТА •	I
3	АИМ	VIII
4	АКМОЛИНСК •	VI
5	АКТЮБИНСК •	VI
6	АЛЕКСАНДРОВСКОЕ	VI
7	АЛДАН •	VI
8	АЛЛАЙХА •	VIII
9	АЛМА-АТА •	VII
10	АНДИЖАН •	VII
11	АРХАНГЕЛЬСК •	I
12	АСКОЛЬД (ОСТРОВ)	VIII
13	АСТРАХАНЬ •	III
14	АША	IV
15	АЯН •	VIII
16	БАКУ •	III
17	БАЛЫЧИГАН •	VIII
18	БЕЛОМОРСК •	I
19	БЕЛУШЬЕ	I
20	БЕРЕЗОВО	V
21	БИРОБИДЖАН •	IX
22	БОДАЙБО •	VI
23	БОРОВИЧИ	II
24	БУРЕЯ •	IX
25	БЮГЮКЕ	V
26	ВАНЗ	I
27	ВАЙГАЧ (ОСТРОВ)	I
28	ВЕЛЬСК •	I
29	ВЕРЕЩАГИНО	V
30	ВЕРХОЯНСК •	VIII
31	ВЕРХНЕ-ИМБАТСКОЕ	V
32	ВЕРХНЕ-УРАЛЬСК	IV
33	ВЕРХНИЙ УФАЛЕЙ •	IV
34	ВЕСЛЯНА	I
35	ВИЛЮЙСК •	VI
36	ВИТИМ •	VI
37	ВОЛОГДА •	II
38	ВОЛХОВ	II
39	ВОРКУТА •	I
40	ВЫТЕГРА •	I
41	ГОРАЛИ	I
42	ГОРЬКИЙ •	II
43	ДЖЕЗКАЗГАН •	VII
44	ДНЕПРОПЕТРОВСК •	II
45	ЕЛАБУГА	II
46	ЕРОФЕЙ ПАВЛОВИЧ •	VI
47	ЖИГАНСК	VI
48	ЗАЯРСК	VI
49	ЗЕМЛЯ ФРАНЦА ИОСИФА •	I
50	ЗЫРЯНКА	VIII
51	ИВАНОВО	II
52	ИВДЕЛЬ •	IV
53	ИЖЕВСК •	II
54	ИЗВЕСТКОВЫЙ	VIII
55	ИМАН	VII
56	ИРГИЗ	VII
57	ИРКУТСК •	VI
58	ИШИМБАЙ •	IV
59	КАГАН	VII
60	КАЗАЛИНСК	VII
61	КАЗАНЬ •	II
62	КАМЧАТКА •	VIII
63	КАНДАЛАКША •	I
64	КАРАБАШ	IV
65	КАРАГАНДА •	VI
66	КАРАКАС	VII
67	КАРАУЛ	V
68	КАРГОПОЛЬ •	I
69	КАШИН	II
70	КЕМЕРОВО •	VI
71	КЗЫЛ-ОРДА	VII
72	КИЗЕЛ •	II
73	КИРОВ (ВЯТКА)	II
74	КНЯЖ-ПОГОСТ	I
75	КОЖВА	I
76	КОКЧЕТАВ	I
77	КОЛБАШЕВО	V
78	КОЛЫМА •	VIII
79	КОМАНДОРСКИЕ О-ВА •	VIII
80	КОМСОМОЛЬСК •	IX
81	КОНДОПОГА	I
82	КОПЕЙСК •	IV
83	КОСТРОМА	II
84	КОТЛАС •	I
85	КРАСНОВОДСК	IV
86	КРАСНОТУРИНСК	IV
87	КРАСНОЯРСК •	V
88	КУЗНЕЦК	VI
89	КУЙБЫШЕВ •	II
90	КУЛОЙ	I
91	КУНГУР •	II
92	КУРГАН-ТЮБЕ •	VII
93	КУРИЛЬСКИЕ ОСТРОВА •	VIII
94	КУРЬЯ	I
95	КУСТАНАЙ •	VI
96	КЫЗЫЛ	V
97	КЮСЮР	VIII
98	ЛЕНИНГРАД •	II
99	ЛЕНИНОГОРСК	VI
100	МАГДАГАЧИ	VIII
101	МАГНИТОГОРСК •	IV
102	МАРИИНСК •	VI
103	МАЙОР-КРЕСТ	VIII
104	МАХАЧКАЛА	III
105	МЕДВЕЖЬЕГОРСК •	I
106	МЕЗЕНЬ	I
107	МИАСС •	IV
108	МИРНОЕ	V
109	МОЛОТОВ • (ПЕРМЬ)	II
110	МОЛОТОВСК	I
111	МОНЧЕГОРСК	I
112	МОРШАНСК	II
113	МОСКВА •	II
114	НАЛЬЧИК	III
115	НАРЬЯН-МАР •	I
116	НИКОЛАЕВСК •	VI
117	НИКОПОЛЬ	II
118	НИЖНИЕ КРЕСТЫ •	VIII
119	НИЖНЕ-ТАМБОВСК.	VIII
120	НИЖНИЙ ТАГИЛ •	IV
121	НОВАЯ ЗЕМЛЯ •	I
122	Н.ШАДРИНО	VI
123	НОВОСИБИРСК •	VI
124	НОРДВИК	I
125	НОРИЛЬСК •	V
126	ОЖОГИНО	VIII
127	ОЛЁКМИНСК •	VI
128	ОМСК •	VI
129	ОРСК •	IV
130	ОСТАШКОВ	II
131	ПАХТА-АРАЛ	VII
132	ПЕНЗА	II
133	ПЕТРОЗАВОДСК •	I
134	ПЕТРОПАВЛОВСК	VI
135	ПЕЧОРА •	I
136	ПЛЕСЕЦК	I
137	ПОДКАМ.ТУНГУСКА	V
138	ПОКУР	VI
139	ПОКЧА	I
140	ПРОКОПЬЕВСК	VI
141	РАМЕНСКОЕ	II
142	РЕВДА	IV
143	РЕЖ	IV
144	РУГОЗЕРО	I
145	САВИНОБОР	I
146	САЛЕХАРД •	V
147	САЛЬЯНЫ	III
148	САМА	IV
149	САРАНСК-ПОТЬМА	II
150	САХАЛИН •	IX
151	СВЕРДЛОВСК •	IV
152	СВИРЬСТРОЙ	II
153	СЕГЕЖА	I
154	СЕЙЧАН •	VIII
155	СЕМИПАЛАТИНСК •	VI
156	СОЛИКАМСК •	II
157	СОЛОВЕЦКИЕ ОСТРОВА •	I
158	СОРТАВАЛА	I
159	СРЕДНЕКОЛЫМСК •	VIII
160	СРЕТИНСК	VI
161	СТАЛИНГРАД •	III
162	СТАЛИНО (ДОНЕЦК) •	II
163	СТАЛИНОГОРСК	II
164	СТАЛИНСК	VI
165	СТАНЧИК	VIII
166	СТАРОДУБ	VI
167	СТОЛБОВОЕ	VIII
168	СУОЯРВИ	I
169	СУХУМИ	III
170	СУЧАН	IX
171	СЫЗРАНЬ	II
172	СЫКТЫВКАР	I
173	ТАВДА	IV
174	ТАЙШЕТ-БРАТСК •	VI
175	ТАШКЕНТ	VII
176	ТБИЛИСИ	III
177	ТЕКЮЛЯК	VIII
178	ТЕТЮШИ	II
179	ТИКСИ	V
180	ТИХВИН	II
181	ТОБОЛЬСК •	VI
182	ТОТЬМА •	I
183	ТОМСК •	VI
184	ТУЛА	II
185	ТУРА	V
186	ТУРИНСК •	IV
187	ТУРКЕСТАН	VII
188	ТУРУХАНСК	V
189	ТЮМЕНЬ •	VI
190	УГЛИЧ	II
191	УЛЬЯНОВСК	II
192	УЛАН-УДЭ	VI
193	УМАНЬ	II
194	УРАЛЬСК	IV
195	УСТЬ-ВОРКУТА	I
196	УСТЬ-ВЫМЬ	I
197	УСТЬ-КАМЕНОГОРСК •	VI
198	УСТЬ-КАМЧАТСКИЙ •	VIII
199	УСТЬ-КУЛОМ	I
200	УСТЬ-МИЛЬ	VIII
201	УСТЬ-ПОРТ	V
202	УСТЬ-СРЕДНИКАН	VIII
203	УСТЬ-УСА	I
204	УСТЬ-УХТА •	I
205	УСТЬ-ШУГОР	I
206	УФА •	IV
207	ФЕРГАНА	VII
208	ФРУНЗЕ	VII
209	ХАБАРОВСК •	IX
210	ХОЛМОГОРЫ	I
211	ХОНУ	VIII
212	ЧАРДЖОУ	VII
213	ЧЕЛКАР	VII
214	ЧЕЛЯБИНСК •	IV
215	ЧИТА •	VI
216	ЧКАЛОВ (ОРЕНБУРГ)	IV
217	ЧУСОВОЙ	IV
218	ШАДРИНСК	IV
219	ЩЕРБАКОВ	I
220	ЭКИБАСТУЗ-УГОЛЬ	VII
221	ЯКУТСК •	V
222	ЯРОСЛАВЛЬ	II

ПРИМЕЧАНИЕ:

• – группа ИТЛ, ИТК и др. учреждений ГУЛАГа от 2-х до 5-и и более

IV – регион (зона) ГУЛАГа

Суточный паёк зэка в ГУЛАГе содержал от 1300 до 3000 калорий

В ГУЛАГе зэки были разделены по категориям режима – материальным и психологическим условиям. Режим вытравливал из человека его индивидуальность и превращал в робота с максимальной производительностью труда.

Note:

• – denotes a group of ITL, ITK or other penal institutions of the Gulag (two to five or more).

iv – a region (zone) of the Gulag [see map on previous pages].

The daily ration of a convict in the Gulag had a nutritional value of 1,300–3,000 calories.

Convicts in the Gulag were divided by the regime into categories – material and psychological conditions. The regime etched away all traces of individuality and turned people into robots with the highest labour productivity.

* *komandirovka* – 'business trip, assignment', a place outside a prison camp where convicts worked (construction site, lumber mill, etc.).

БОЛЬШЕВИКИ ПЕРВЫМИ В МИРЕ СОЗДАЛИ СИСТЕМУ РАБСКИХ ТРУДОВЫХ АРМИЙ ГУЛАГА, ЧЕГО, КАК ИЗВЕСТНО, НЕ БЫЛО ПРИ ЦАРИЗМЕ. В СОЛОВЕЦКОМ ЛАГЕРЕ НАЧАЛИСЬ ЭКСПЕ-РИМЕНТЫ ПО „РАСЧЕЛОВЕЧИВАНИЮ" ЛЮДЕЙ САМЫМИ ЖЕ-СТОКИМИ МЕТОДАМИ В „ЛАГЕРНУЮ ПЫЛЬ"...

The Bolsheviks were the first in the world to create slave-labour armies in the Gulag system, which had not existed in czarist Russia. The Solovki* prison camp was where the experiments in the 'dehumanization' of people began, and where the most brutal methods were used to crush people into 'prison camp dust'...†

* See page 15.
† As well as coping with the harsh realities inside the camps, there was also a considerable shortage of tools in the working zones. It was common for (usually frozen) earth to be dug using bare hands. Workers were forced to improvise their own implements from whatever was at hand, basic picks and hammers were fashioned from stone, metal and wood. Shaped by a combination of work and frostbite, hands quickly became impossible to use with any dexterity, or even to open out flat.

ГУЛАГОВСКАЯ ШУТКА НАД ВНОВЬ ПРИБЫВШИМ ЭТАПОМ ЗАКЛЮЧЁННЫХ „ПОДДАТЬ ПАРА"

ДЛЯ УСПОКОЕНИЯ ПРИБЫВШИХ И ВОЗМУЩАЮЩИХСЯ ДОЛГИМ ОЖИДАНИЕМ В „ОТСТОЙНИКЕ" ПЕРЕД ПРИЁМОМ ЭТАПА В ИТЛ, ЗЭКОВ ПРИ МОРОЗЕ 30-40° ОБЛИВАЛИ С ВЫШКИ ВОДОЙ ИЗ ПОЖАРНОГО ШЛАНГА И ПО УСМОТРЕНИЮ (ПРОИЗВОЛУ) НАЧАЛЬСТВА ЧЕРЕЗ 2-4 ЧАСА ОБЛЕДЕНЕВШИХ ВЕЛИ В ЗОНУ...

A Gulag prank called 'adding steam' being played on newly arrived prisoners.

To pacify the newly arrived prisoners, who expressed their indignation with the long stay in the 'settling tank' before they were let into the camp, they were hosed with water from the watchtower when it was 30° to 40° C below freezing. Two or three hours later – their clothes frozen to their bodies – they might be allowed inside the zone,* depending on the whim of the prison authorities.

* A 'zone' was the prisoners' word for any prison, camp or restricted area where they were made to work (lumbering or mining for example). They referred to the Soviet Union as the 'big zone', believing the Communist Party's power structure to be identical to that of the 'legitimate thieves' who ruled the 'little zone' – the Gulag (see page 202).

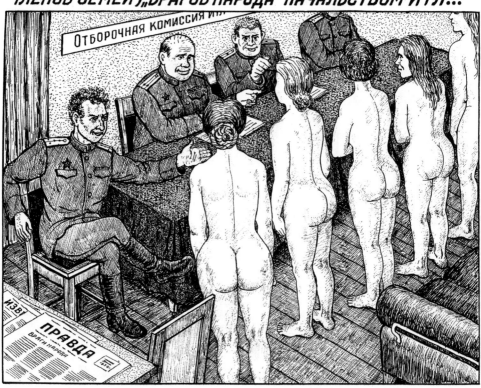

ЖЕНЩИНЫ-„ВРАГИ НАРОДА" ПРОХОДИЛИ ОСМОТР ПЕРЕД ОТБОРОЧНОЙ КОМИССИЕЙ ПО РАСПРЕДЕЛЕНИЮ НА РАБОТЫ ГОЛЫМИ. ПОНРАВИВШИХСЯ ЖЕНЩИН НАПРАВЛЯЛИ В ХОЗОБСЛУГУ ЛАГЕРЯ, ГДЕ ОНИ СТАНОВИЛИСЬ ЛЮБОВНИЦАМИ, ПРИ ОТКАЗЕ НАПРАВЛЯЛИ НА ЛЕСОПОВАЛ И ДР. ТЯЖЕЛЫЕ ФИЗИЧЕСКИЕ РАБОТЫ ИЛИ САЖАЛИ В ШИЗО ЗА „ПРОВИННОСТЬ" И МОРИЛИ ГОЛОДОМ И Т.П.

Prison authorities select slave mistresses from newly arrived Family Members of Traitors of the Motherland.*
Sign on the wall reads: **'Selection Board'**. The newspapers on the desk are: *Izvestiya* and *Pravda*.

Women 'enemies of the people' appeared before the job assignment selection board naked. Those who caught the eye of the board members were sent to in-house jobs in prison camps and became the board members' concubines. If the women refused, they were assigned to lumbering or other hard labour, or locked up in isolation cells (for 'violations'), starved, etc.

* During the Great Purge (1936-1938), NKVD Order Number 00486 of 15th August 1937, allowed the wives and children of 'enemies of the people' (Family Members of Traitors of the Motherland) to be imprisoned in labour camps. Those under fifteen years old were placed in special orphanages for children of 'enemies of the people'.

ОБЫСК-„ШМОН" ПРИБЫВШЕГО ЭТАПА ЗАКЛЮЧЁННЫХ...
В КАЖДОМ ИТЛ В ТЕЧЕНИЕ СУТОК ПРОИЗВОДИЛИСЬ ОБЫСКИ-
ИСКАЛИ ЗАПРЕЩЕННОЕ, СЧИТАЛИ ЗЭКОВ, ВЫЯВЛЯЯ ФАК-
ТЫ ПОБЕГА, СМЕРТИ, УБИЙСТВ...

Sign on the left reads: **'Rights and Responsibilities of the Prisoner'**; sign on the right reads: **'The Gulag of the Ministry of Internal Affairs of the USSR is the Educator of Pris[oners]'**.

The *shmon** of the newly arrived…

Throughout the day, each prison camp organised searches. The guards looked for illegal items, counted the prisoners, and established the facts of escape attempts, deaths and murders.

* *shmon* – 'search' in criminal argot.

Life

НЕСМОТРЯ НА АДСКИЕ УСЛОВИЯ В ГУЛАГЕ, ЖИЗНЬ ВСЕ ЖЕ БРАЛА СВОЁ... ЛЮ-
ДИ ВЛЮБЛЯЛИСЬ, ПИСАЛИ ПИСЬМА, ПРИЗНАВАЛИСЬ В ЛЮБВИ... ПОСЛЕ ОСВО-
БОЖДЕНИЯ ЖЕНИЛИСЬ, РАСТИЛИ ДЕТЕЙ...

Sign on the building reads: **'Glory to the Communist Party of the Soviet Union!'**.

Despite the inferno that the Gulag was, life went on. People fell in love, wrote notes to each other, confessed their feelings. After they were released,[*] they got married and brought up children.

* Even after being granted their freedom, for various reasons inmates often found it difficult to leave the Gulag. For some the long journey home from their remote exiles was simply too daunting; for others too much time had elapsed, and they felt they couldn't rebuild their 'past' lives outside the system; still others found themselves in positions of power that they could never have achieved outside camp circumstances – they might become 'free workers' or even guards; some were released but forbidden to leave.

УГОЛОВНИК „БУГОР" ДАЕТ УКАЗАНИЕ „ВОРОВСКИМ МУЖИКАМ"...

ПОСЛЕ УКАЗА ПВС СССР ОТ 06.07.1947Г. В ИТЛ ГУЛАГА ИЗ ОСУЖДЕННЫХ ОБРАЗОВАЛИСЬ ТРИ КРУПНЫХ „МАСТИ" (ПРИНАДЛЕЖНОСТЬ К ОПРЕДЕЛЕННОМУ ПРЕСТУПНОМУ КОНТИНГЕНТУ): „ВОРЫ", СУКИ" И „МУЖИКИ". ПОСЛЕ АДМИНИСТРАЦИИ ИТЛ ГУЛАГА, 2-й ВЛАСТЬЮ" БЫЛИ „ВОРЫ" И „СУКИ", У КОТОРЫХ „МУЖИКИ" БЫЛИ В ПРИТЕСНЕННОМ ПОЛОЖЕНИИ, В ТОМ ЧИСЛЕ И „ВРАГИ НАРОДА". АВТОРИТЕТНЫЕ УГОЛОВНИКИ НЕ РАБОТАЛИ, ИМЕЯ „ВОРОВСКИХ МУЖИКОВ"- ЗЭКОВ, КОТОРЫЕ ОТДАВАЛИ ИМ ЧАСТЬ ПРОЦЕНТОВ ВЫРАБОТКИ И ЗАРАБОТКА ЗА ТО, ЧТО ОНИ ОБЕРЕГАЛИ ИХ ОТ ПРИТЕСНЕНИЙ СО СТОРОНЫ ДР. УГОЛОВНИКОВ. АДМИНИСТРАЦИЯ ИТЛ ГУЛАГА УМЫШЛЕННО СТАВИЛА НАД БРИГАДАМИ „МУЖИКОВ" БРИГАДИРАМИ „БУГРОВ" – УГОЛОВНИКОВ ДЛЯ ОСУЩЕСТВЛЕНИЯ ЗВЕРСКОЙ ЭКСПЛУАТАЦИИ...

A *bugor** gives orders to his *muzhiks*.†

After the Presidium of the Supreme Council decree of 6th July 1947, three large 'suits' (groups) of criminals were formed: thieves, 'bitches', and *muzhiks*. The second echelon of power of the Gulag, underneath the administration, were the thieves and 'bitches',‡ who oppressed the *muzhiks*. The 'enemies of the people' shared the fate of the *muzhiks*. Authoritative criminals did not work. *Muzhiks* wrote off some of their daily work quota in their favour, in exchange for protection from other criminals. The administration of the Gulag intentionally appointed *bugors* as foremen of *muzhik* crews to facilitate the brutal exploitation of the latter.

---

* *bugor* – a 'brigadier'. A prisoner (usually a criminal 'authority'), who was placed in charge of a brigade of workers by the administration. They were responsible for their brigade's work quota and were exempt from physical labour.
† *muzhik* – a 'peasant', a low ranking thief.
‡ bitches – criminals who had sided with the authorities, taking trusted positions in the camp to escape its rigours (see page 82).

„ПРИДУРКИ"-ЧАСТЬ ПРИВИЛЕГИРОВАННЫХ ЗЭКОВ...

В ГУЛАГЕ „ПРИДУРКАМИ" НАЗЫВАЛИСЬ ЗЭКИ, ВЫПОЛНЯВШИЕ ВНУТРИХОЗЯЙСТ-
ВЕННЫЕ РАБОТЫ В ИТЛ: ПОВАРА, КУХОННЫЕ РАБОЧИЕ, КЛАДОВЩИКИ, ЭЛЕКТРИКИ,
МОТОРИСТЫ, КУБОВЫЕ, БАНЩИКИ, УБОРЩИКИ ПОМЕЩЕНИЙ И Т.Д. „ПРИДУРКИ" ОСВО-
БОЖДАЛИСЬ ОТ ОБЩИХ РАБОТ НА ШАХТАХ, ЛЕСОЗАГОТОВКАХ И Т.П. ОНИ ОЧЕНЬ ДО-
РОЖИЛИ МЕСТОМ, Т.К. ЭТО ПОЗВОЛЯЛО ИМ ВЫЖИТЬ В АДСКИХ УСЛОВИЯХ...

'Fools' – some of the privileged prisoners.

Pridurki[*] – 'Fools' in the Gulag were prisoners who were employed in jobs within the prison camp: cooks, kitchen workers, warehouse workers, electricians, car mechanics, boiler servicemen, sauna workers, janitors, etc. 'Fools' were free from general labour in mines, lumbering, etc. They cherished their jobs, as they allowed them to survive in otherwise unbearable conditions.

[*] This name is derived from their 'fooling about' – working cushy jobs, rather than doing hard labour. Most were criminals, as they were deemed to be 'socially acceptable', unlike the 'politicals' (after 1930 camp authorities were forbidden to give any administrative work to political prisoners).

В ГУЛАГЕ ЗЭКИ-„ВРАГИ НАРОДА", НЕ ВЫДЕРЖАВ ИЗУВЕРСТВА И САДИЗМ, УМЫШЛЕННО БРОСАЛИСЬ В ЗАПРЕТНУЮ ЗОНУ...

ГУЛАГ - ЛУЧШЕЕ ВОСПИТАТЕЛЬНОЕ УЧРЕЖДЕНИЕ ПРЕСТУПНИКОВ ВО ВСЁМ МИРЕ.
Министр МВД
Л.П.БЕРИЯ

БРИГАДИРАМИ „БУГРАМИ" НАД ЗЭКАМИ „ВРАГАМИ НАРОДА"В ГУЛАГЕ ЧАСТО НАЗНАЧАЛИ УГОЛОВНИКОВ-УРОК, И ЧЕМ ОНИ БОЛЬШЕ ЗВЕРСТВОВАЛИ, ТЕМ БОЛЬШЕ ЭТО УСТРАИВАЛО АДМИНИСТРАЦИЮ ЛАГЕРЯ... УРКИ" ПО СВОЕМУ САМОДУРСТВУ ПОЛНЕЙШЕМУ ПРОИЗВОЛУ ЗАСТАВЛЯЛИ ЗЭКОВ, ПОД УГРОЗОЙ ИЗБИЕНИЯ И СМЕРТИ: „ГАРНИР ХАВАТЬ"-ЕСТЬ ЧЕЛОВЕЧЕСКИЕ ИСПРАЖНЕНИЯ, ПИТЬ МОЧУ, СОСАТЬ ПОЛОВОЙ ЧЛЕН, ЦЕЛОВАТЬ И ЛИЗАТЬ „ОЧКО"-АНАЛЬНОЕ ОТВЕРСТИЕ, А ТАКЖЕ ЗАСТАВЛЯЛИ РАБОТАТЬ БЕЗ ОТДЫХА (ВЫХОДНЫХ) ПО 12-16 ЧАСОВ, ОТБИРАЛИ ПОСЫЛКИ С ПРОДУКТАМИ, ПАЁК, ХОРОШУЮ ОДЕЖДУ, ОБУВЬ, ПРЕДМЕТЫ... НА ЖАЛОБЫ ЗЭКОВ НАЧАЛЬСТВО ГУЛАГА НЕ ОБРАЩАЛО НИКАКОГО ВНИМАНИЯ, И ВСЕ ЭТО ПРОИСХОДИЛО С ИХ СОГЛАСИЯ. ЖАЛОБЩИКИ НАКАЗЫВАЛИСЬ.

Having had enough torture and sadistic treatment in the Gulag, the 'enemies of the people' intentionally entered the forbidden zone.*
Text on the wall reads: '**The Gulag is the best correctional institution for criminals in the world.' Minister of Internal Affairs, L.P. Beria'**.

In the Gulag, *bugors*, the foremen of the prisoner brigades made up of 'enemies of the people', were often *urkas* – authoritative criminals. The crueller they were, the more it satisfied the prison administration. *Urkas* exercised their power by making prisoners, under penalty of severe beating or death, 'gobble the garnish', i.e. eat human excrement, drink urine, perform oral sex, kiss and lick the 'cornhole', i.e. the anus. *Urkas* also forced them to work without days off for twelve to sixteen hours, took away parcels with food, daily rations, clothing, footwear and personal possessions. The Gulag authorities ignored the prisoners' complaints. Everything happened with their consent. Those who complained were punished.

* 'First they disentangled Romashev from the wire… When nothing more held the body, Shved and the warder held the body still for a moment, head down, and then let it drop, and we heard Romashev hit the ground with a sickening thud. A low hiss, half sigh and half exclamation travelled through the compound. And then at once a dreadful din broke out – shouts, protests, hysterics almost. I myself saw several cons – old Kolyma and Vorkuta hands – break down in tears. Torture and starvation had never managed to squeeze tears out of men like this, but now they wept with mortification and impotent rage.' Anatoly Marchenko, *My Testimony*, 1969.

ВЫВОД ЗА ЗОНУ ИТЛ ПОД КОНВОЕМ АРТИСТОВ-ЗЭКОВ, В ТОМ ЧИСЛЕ И ЗАСЛУЖЕННЫХ, ДЛЯ ДАЧИ КОНЦЕРТА В МЕСТНОМ ТАЁЖНОМ ПОСЕЛ-КОВОМ КЛУБЕ. ВО ВРЕМЯ КОНЦЕРТА ОХРАНА С ОРУЖИЕМ И СЛУЖЕБ-НОЙ СОБАКОЙ РАСПОЛАГАЛИСЬ НА СЦЕНЕ ЗА КУЛИСАМИ И В ЗАЛЕ...

Guards take convicted musicians, including *Zasluzhenny* Artists* outside the prison camp to give a concert in a taiga village. Guards with guns and watchdogs were present during the concert – on the stage, behind the stage and in the audience.

* *Zasluzhenny* Artist (also translated as Meritorious, Merited, Distinguished, or Honorary Artist) – was an honorary title in the Soviet Union which was awarded for exceptional achievements in the performing arts.

ПОЁТ КРЕПОСТНАЯ АКТРИСА ИТЛ ГУЛАГА: -РОССИЯ ВОЛЬ-НАЯ, СТРАНА ПРЕКРАСНАЯ, СОВЕТСКИЙ КРАЙ МОЯ ЗЕМЛЯ...

– ОТКУДА ЭТА ПЕВИЧКА? ХОРОШО СТЕРВА ПОЕТ...
-ИЗ ЛЕНИНГРАДСКОГО ТЕАТРА,ПО 58=Й! ИХ К ИВАНОВУ ТРОИХ ЗАСЛУЖЕННЫХ ПРИГНАЛИ,
ПРИШЛОСЬ ЗА НЕЁ ПЯТЬ ЗЭЧЕК ОТДАТЬ: ТРИ ПОРТНИХИ, БУХГАЛТЕРШУ И ПОВАРИХУ,
КОТОРАЯ НА ВОЛЕ В РЕСТОРАНЕ РАБОТАЛА, НО ТЕПЕРЬ У НАС ЕСТЬ СВОЯ АРТИСТКА...

A slave singer of the Gulag prison camp sings: Russia is the land of freedom / Beautiful land / My land, the Soviet land.

'Where's she from? The bitch knows how to sing!'
'She's from a theatre in Leningrad, doing time under Article 58.* Ivanov got three of them, all "Honoured Artists."
I had to give him five cons for her: three seamstresses, one accountant, and a cook – she worked in a restaurant
out of prison. And now we have our very own singer.'

* Article 58 of the Penal Code of the Russian Soviet Federative Socialist Republic of 25th February 1927, dealt with anti-Soviet activities,
counter-revolutionary activities, treason, espionage, undermining of state industry and transport (sabotage), terrorism, non-reporting
of counter-revolutionary activities, etc. Prisoners convicted under Article 58 were known as 'political prisoners', their sentences were
usually long (up to twenty-five years) and could be extended without trial.

ВНУТРИЛАГЕРНАЯ ВОЙНА МЕЖДУ „ИДЕЙНЫМИ ВОРАМИ В ЗАКОНЕ" И ОТКОЛОВШИМИСЯ ВОРАМИ „СУКАМИ"...

ПОСЛЕ УКАЗА ПВС СССР ОТ 06.07.1947г. (ГДЕ СРОКИ ЗА КРАЖИ, ГРАБЕЖИ, РАЗБОИ БЫЛИ ОПРЕДЕЛЕНЫ ДО 20-25 ЛЕТ) ПРОИЗОШЕЛ РАСКОЛ В УГОЛОВНОМ МИРЕ. ЧАСТЬ „ВОРОВ В ЗАКОНЕ," ЧТОБЫ ВЫЖИТЬ В УСЛОВИЯХ ГУЛАГА, СТАЛА РАБОТАТЬ, И ИМ АДМИНИСТРАЦИЯ ИТЛ ДЕЛАЛА ЗАЧЕТЫ 1=3, Т.Е. ПО ИСТЕЧЕНИИ 1/3 СРОКА ЗЭК ОБРЕТАЛ СВОБОДУ. ИДЕЙНЫЕ „ВОРЫ В ЗАКОНЕ," (КОТОРЫЕ, СОГЛАСНО ВОРОВСКИМ НЕ ПИСАННЫМ ЗАКОНАМ И ПРАВИЛАМ, ОТКАЗЫВАЛИСЬ ОТ РАБОТЫ) СТАЛИ НАЗЫВАТЬ РАБОТАЮЩИХ ВОРОВ „СУКАМИ"- ПРЕДАТЕЛЯМИ „ВОРОВСКИХ ЗАКОНОВ," И МЕЖДУ НИМИ НАЧАЛАСЬ НЕПРИМИРИМАЯ ВРАЖДА. В ИТЛ ГУЛАГА БЫЛИ СЛУЧАИ, КОГДА ПРИ СХВАТКАХ ИДЕЙНЫХ „ВОРОВ В ЗАКОНЕ" И „СУК" ПОГИБАЛО ПО 50 И БОЛЕЕ ЗЭКОВ. НАЧАЛЬСТВО ГУЛАГА ДЕЙСТВЕННЫХ МЕР НЕ ПРИНИМАЛО...

Internal warfare between 'idealist, legitimate' thieves, and traitor 'bitch' thieves.

After the Presidium of the Supreme Council decree of 6th July 1947, which introduced a punishment for theft and robbery of twenty to twenty-five years imprisonment, the criminal world divided into two camps. In order to survive in the Gulag, some of the 'legitimate' thieves began to work. The prison administration introduced a system of incentives for them, which was called 'one for three'. It was possible for the prisoner to be discharged after only a third of his imprisonment term had elapsed. The 'idealist', 'legitimate' thieves, who refused to work (in accordance with their thieves' code of honour), called the working thieves 'bitches' and traitors to the code. Relentless warfare broke out between them. There were incidents in the history of the Gulag prison camps when fifty or more prisoners were killed in fights[*] between 'legitimate' thieves and 'bitches'. The Gulag authorities did not take action against such fights.

[*] See page 198.

В ГУЛАГЕ БЛАТАРИ-„ВОРЫ В ЗАКОНЕ" БЫЛИ В ПРИВИЛЕГИРО-ВАННОМ ПОЛОЖЕНИИ, КАК СОВРЕМЕННЫЕ БЮРОКРАТЫ...

Уголовники В ГУЛАГЕ БЫЛИ ПО ПОЛОЖЕНИЮ НА ТРИ ПОРЯДКА ВЫШЕ „ВРА-ГОВ НАРОДА". АВТОРИТЕТНЫЕ, НЕ ОДНОКРАТНО СУДИМЫЕ „ВОРЫ В ЗАКОНЕ", КАК ПРАВИЛО, НЕ РАБОТАЛИ, МЕЛКИЕ ВОРЫ-„ШЕСТЁРКИ" БЫЛИ У НИХ В УСЛУЖЕ-НИИ, А ЗЭКИ БЫТОВИКИ-„ВОРОВСКИЕ МУЖИКИ", ОТДАВАЛИ ПРОЦЕНТЫ ВЫРА-БОТКИ. УГОЛОВНИКИ ПОМОГАЛИ УНИЧТОЖАТЬ „ВРАГОВ НАРОДА" В ИТЛ ГУЛАГА...

'Legitimate' thieves in the Gulag were as privileged as modern-day bureaucrats.

Criminal prisoners[*] in the Gulag ranked three times higher than the 'enemies of the people'. Authoritative or 'legitimate' thieves with numerous previous convictions usually did not work. They had *shesterkas*[†] (underlings or minions) working for them. The *muzhiks* wrote off some of their daily work quota in favour of the authoritative thieves. Criminals helped eradicate the 'enemies of the people' in the Gulag prison camps.

[*] Here Baldaev clearly shows the tattoos that the criminals used to display their rank and history. Tattoos were also used as a statement against the authorities: '… there wasn't a clear spot on his whole face. On one cheek he had "Lenin was a butcher" and on the other it continued: "Millions are suffering because of him". Under his eyes was: "Khrushchev, Brezhnev, Voroshilov are butchers". On his pale, skinny neck a hand had been tattooed in black ink. It was gripping his throat and on the back of the hand were the letters CPSU, while the middle finger, ending on his adam's apple, was labelled KGB.' Anatoly Marchenko, *My Testimony*, 1969.
[†] *shesterkas* – literally 'sixes'. The six is the lowest card in a standard Russian thirty-six card deck.

- КУДА ЛАПУ ТЯНЕШЬ, КОНТРА! ЧЕРЕЗ НЕДЕЛЮ ДУБА ДАШЬ, А ЕМУ ЕЩЁ ЛЕКАРСТВО ДАЙ...
ГЛАВНЫМ СПЕЦИАЛИСТОМ В БОЛЬНИЦАХ ИТЛ БЫЛ МЕДБРАТ ИЗ З/К. ЕСЛИ ОН БЫЛ ИЗ
БЫТОВИКОВ, ТО СНАБЖАЛ ЛЕКАРСТВАМИ И ПРОДУКТАМИ УГОЛОВНИКОВ-БАЛОВАННЫХ ДЕТЕЙ
КРАСНОГО КРЕМЛЯ, А „ВРАГИ НАРОДА" ИНТЕЛЛИГЕНТЫ, РАБОЧИЕ И Т.Д. БЫЛИ ОБДЕЛЕНЫ...

Signs on the wall read (left to right): **'Do not spit on the floor!'**, graffiti added underneath: **'But spit on the
Communist Party!'**; **'Wash your hands before you eat!'**; **'Brush your teeth!'**. The patient in the nearest bed holds
a copy of the newspaper **'*Pravda*'**.

'Keep your paws to yourself, counter-revolutionary! You're going to kick the bucket in a week anyway, so you
don't need medicine.'

The chief medical specialist in prison camp hospitals was a nurse, who was also a prisoner. If he was one of
the *bytoviks*,[*] he brought medicine and food to other criminals, the spoiled children of the Red Kremlin. The
'enemies of the people' – the intelligentsia, workers, etc. – were deprived of such 'luxuries'.

[*] *bytovik* – a criminal prisoner. An inmate who has been sentenced for a criminal act (murder for example), but is not a professional
criminal and doesn't actually belong to the 'true' criminal world.

ДЕВУШКИ И ЖЕНЩИНЫ НЕ ИМЕЙТЕ ПОЛОВЫ
СВЯЗЕЙ С ЛЕСБИЯНКАМИ-ВАС ЖДУТ ДОМА

БИЧЁМ ЖЕНСКИХ ИТЛ-ИТК ГУЛАГА-УИТЛК-УМЗ И СОВРЕМЕННОГО
УИТУ ЯВЛЯЮТСЯ „КОБЛЫ"-АКТИВНЫЕ МУЖЕПОДОБНЫЕ ЛЕСБИ-
ЯНКИ,ИЗ-ЗА КОТОРЫХ ПРОИСХОДЯТ ССОРЫ И ДРАКИ МЕЖДУ ПАС-
СИВНЫМИ ЛЕСБИЯНКАМИ...

Text at the top reads: **'Girls and women, do not engage in sexual affairs with lesbians! Someone is waiting for you at home'**.

The scourge of women's camps in the Gulag system, as well as modern-day prisons, were *koblas* – active, masculine lesbians. They were the cause of skirmishes and fights between passive lesbians.

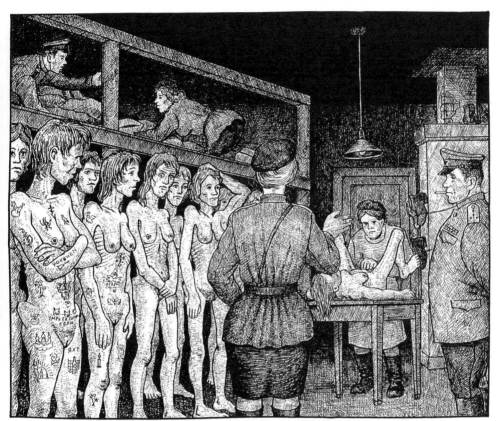

НОЧНОЙ ОБЫСК-«ШМОН» В ЖЕНСКОМ БАРАКЕ ИТУ ГУЛАГА С ЦЕЛЬЮ ИЗЪЯТИЯ У ВОРОВОК И ИХ КОДЛЫ-«ЖУЧЕК» НАРКОТИКОВ, НОЖЕЙ, ОПАСНЫХ БРИТВ, СПИРТНОГО, ПОРНОГРАФИИ И Т.Д. ТАКИЕ ОБЫСКИ В ГУЛАГЕ ПРОВОДИЛИСЬ РЕГУЛЯРНО В ЖЕНСКИХ И МУЖСКИХ ЗОНАХ.

A night search in a women's barrack of the Gulag in order to confiscate drugs, knives, razor blades, alcohol, pornographic materials, etc. from female thieves and their *zhuchkas*.* Such searches were common in both the men's and women's prisons of the Gulag.

* *zhuchkas* – small dog or mongrel; the name given to female accomplices.

Death

ВЫБРОС ТРУПОВ ЗАКЛЮЧЁННЫХ-УБИТЫХ И УМЕРШИХ В ТРЮМАХ ПАРОХОДА-В ОХОТСКОЕ МОРЕ ПРИ ЭТАПЕ С МАТЕРИКА В БУХТУ НАГАЕВО – ГОР. МАГАДАН...

Throwing prisoners bodies overboard. They either died or were killed in ship's holds[*] during deportation from the mainland to Nagaevo Bay in Magadan, in the Sea of Okhotsk.

---

* Hoses were often used by the guards to control their human cargo. In *Kolyma Tales* Varlam Shalamov recalls how on 5th December 1947, this method was employed to put a stop to 3,000 convicts who, during their journey to Magadan, had mutinied aboard the steamship *Kim*. At 40° C below freezing, those that didn't die suffered third- and fourth-degree frostbite.

„УРАЛЛАГ" КАРАБАШ. СБРОС ТРУПОВ З/К В СТВОЛ СТАРОЙ ШАХ-
ТЫ. ТАКИХ „МОГИЛЬНИКОВ" НА НЕОБЪЯТНЫХ ПРОСТОРАХ ГУЛАГА
БЫЛИ СОТНИ. И ЭТО ДО СИХ ПОР „ГОСТАЙНА" КОММУНИСТОВ...

Urallag-Karabash. Bodies of dead prisoners being dumped into a shaft of an old mine. There were hundreds of such 'sepulchres' (tomb or burial vaults) throughout the limitless territories of the Gulag. This fact is still regarded as 'top secret' by the Communists.*

* All the drawings in this book were made by Baldaev during the Communist period. Following the failed coup of August 1991, realising that the end of the regime was imminent, the security forces of the KGB and MVD attempted to destroy incriminating evidence held in their archive.

УКЛАДКА ТРУПОВ „ВРАГОВ НАРОДА" В „АММОНАЛЬНИК"...

„АММОНАЛЬНИКИ"-ЭТО ЯМЫ, ОБРАЗОВАННЫЕ В ВЕЧНОЙ МЕРЗЛО-
ТЕ ПУТЁМ ПРИМЕНЕНИЯ ВЗРЫВЧАТКИ: ДИНАМИТА, ТОЛУОЛА
И АММОНАЛА, ВМЕСТИМОСТЬЮ ОТ ДЕСЯТКА ДО СОТЕН ТРУПОВ.

Dumping of the corpses of 'enemies of the people' in an *ammonalnik*.

Ammonalniks were pits made in the permafrost using dynamite, TNT, or ammonal explosives. They accommodated tens or hundreds of thousands of dead bodies.[*]

[*] 'The mountain had been laid bare and transformed into a gigantic stage for a camp mystery play. A grave, a mass prisoner grave, a stone pit stuffed full with undecaying corpses from 1938 was sliding down the side of the hill, revealing the secret of Kolyma... All of our loved ones who died in Kolyma, all those who were shot, beaten to death, sucked dry by starvation, can still be recognised even after tens of years. There were no gas furnaces in Kolyma. The corpses wait in stone, in the permafrost.' Varlam Shalamov, *Kolyma Tales*, 1980.

В ИТЛ ГУЛАГА ПОСЛЕ ОЧЕРЕДНОЙ УКЛАДКИ ТРУПОВ- „ДУБАРЕЙ","ЖМУРИКОВ" В ШТАБЕЛЯ У „КАНДЕЯ"...

В СЕВЕРНЫХ ИТЛ ГУЛАГА: КРАСНОЯРСКОМ КРАЕ, КОМИ АССР, НА КОЛЫМЕ И ДР. РЕГИОНАХ, ПО ПРИЧИНЕ БОЛЬШОЙ СМЕРТНОСТИ ЗЭКОВ ОТ ТЯЖЕЛОЙ РАБОТЫ, НЕДОЕДАНИЯ, БОЛЕЗНЕЙ И ВНУТРИЛАГЕРНОГО ТЕРРОРА, ТРУПЫ В ЗИМНЕЕ ВРЕМЯ ИЗ-ЗА ТРУДНОСТИ ЗАХОРОНЕНИЯ СКЛАДЫВАЛИСЬ В ШТАБЕЛЯ В СВОЕОБРАЗНЫХ „СКЛАДАХ", А С НАСТУПЛЕНИЕМ ВЕСНЫ ЗАХОРАНИВАЛИСЬ БЕЗ ОДЕЖДЫ В „АММОНАЛЬНИКАХ", ТОПИЛИСЬ В БОЛОТАХ И СЖИГАЛИСЬ. „КАНДЕЙ"- КАРЦЕР, ШТРАФНОЙ ИЗОЛЯТОР В САРАЕ ИЛИ ЛЕТНЕЙ ПАЛАТКЕ, КОТОРЫЙ НЕ ОТАПЛИВАЛСЯ ПРИ МОРОЗАХ 30-60°..

The Gulag Corrective Prison Camp after stacking corpses '*dubars*', '*zhmuriks*'* by the *kandey*.
Text on the building reads: '*Kandey.* **Long Live Communism and Death to Its Enemies!**'.

In the northern prison camps of the Gulag system – Krasnoyarsk Region, Komi ASSR, Kolyma and others – many prisoners died from hard work, malnourishment, disease and inhumane treatment. Because burying them was problematic, the bodies were stacked like logs. When spring came, the bodies were buried naked in *ammonalniks*, sunk in swamps, or burned. The *kandey* is a slang word for the isolation cell. Barns or tents were sometimes used as isolation cells. They were unheated even when the temperatures outside fell as low as 30º to 60º C below freezing.

* *dubars, zhmuriks* – various slang terms for the dead (eg: 'stiff').

ОТПРАВКА „ЖМУРИКОВ" НА ПОСЕЛЕНИЕ В СЕВЕРНЫЙ ЛЕДОВИ-
ТЫЙ ОКЕАН – УТОПЛЕНИЕ ЗАМОРОЖЕННЫХ ТРУПОВ ЗАКЛЮ-
ЧЕННЫХ   ПРОРУБИ СИБИРСКОЙ РЕКИ.

'Stiffs' being sent to a 'settlement' in the Arctic Ocean. The frozen corpses of prisoners are disposed of
through a hole in the ice of a Siberian river.

Text on signs (left to right) reads: **'Rights and Responsibilities of the Prisoner'**; **'Fuel Warehouse'**; **'Checkpoint No.2'**; **'Forward, to Communism!'**; **'Glory to the Communist Party!'**; **'To Freedom with a Clear Conscience!'**. Portraits at the gate: Karl Marx (left) and Vladimir Lenin (right).

'Brain (skull) punching.' Holes were made in the skulls of (dead) prisoners with a special hammer (a 'puncher') or the pointed end of a crowbar, before they were taken out of the camp to be buried. According to political prisoners of the Gulag, party bureaucrats would stop at no crime, infamous deed, abomination, or lie.[*][†]

* Baldaev is incredulous about this procedure, which was undertaken not to ensure that the victims were dead (this was already obvious), but because the administration wanted them 'double dead' – an outrageous and absurd act.

ИТЕЛЬНО – ТРУДОВЫХ ЛАГЕРЕЙ НА ПРАВАХ ГЛАВКА) ГУЛАГА.
ИАЛЬНЫМ ПРОБОЙНИКОМ – „КОМПОСТЕРОМ" (МОЛОТКОМ) ИЛИ
НЫ ИТЛ ДЛЯ ЗАХОРОНЕНИЯ. ПО МНЕНИЮ БЫВШИХ ПОЛИТЗЭ –
Д КОТОРЫМИ МОГЛИ БЫ ОСТАНОВИТЬСЯ ПАРТОКРАТЫ...

† 'After they had been stacked like timber in an open-sided sled until enough had accumulated for a mass burial in the camp cemetery, they were loaded, naked, onto sledges, heads on the outside, feet inside. Each body bore a wooden tag, a *birka*, tied to the big toe of the right foot, bearing its name and number. Before each sledge left the camp gate, the *nadziratel*, an NKVD officer, took a pickaxe and smashed in each head. This was to ensure that no one got out alive. Once outside the camp, the bodies were dumped into *transeya*, one of several broad ditches dug during summer for this purpose. But as the number of dead mounted, the procedure for making certain they were dead changed. Instead of smashing heads with a pickaxe, the guards used a *szompol*, a thick wire with a sharpened point, which they stuck into each body. Apparently this was easier than swinging a pick.' Edward Buca, *Vorkuta*, 1976.

Hard Labour

ЖЕНЩИНЫ-"ВРАГИ НАРОДА" ОТРАБАТЫВАЮТ В ЛАГЕРЕ СВОЮ „ВИНУ" ПЕРЕД ПАРТИЕЙ И СОВЕТСКИМ НАРОДОМ...

Women 'enemies of the people' work off their 'guilt' before the Communist Party and the Soviet People in the prison camp.

КОММУНИСТЫ – ЯРЫЕ ВРАГИ СВОБОДЫ, ДЕМОКРАТИИ, ВСЕГО ЧЕЛОВЕЧЕСТВА УМЕРТВИЛИ В ЗАСТЕНКАХ НКВД-МГБ И В ГУЛАГЕ МИЛЛИОНЫ ЖЕНЩИН-"КУЛАЧЕК","ВРАГОВ НАРОДА" И ЧСИР ГОЛОДОМ, ХОЛОДОМ, БОЛЕЗНЯМИ И РАБСКИМ ТРУДОМ...

Communists were vehement enemies of freedom, democracy and all humanity. In the prisons of the NKVD-MGB and the Gulag, they were responsible for the deaths of millions of women, *kulachkas*,* 'enemies of the people' and Family Members of Traitors of the Motherland, from starvation, cold, disease and slave labour.

* *kulachka* – the wife of *kulak* (see page 102).

СОДЕРЖАНИЕ ЗЭКОВ-„ВРАГОВ НАРОДА"В ВОЛЧЬИХ ЯМАХ

ЧАСТО ПРИБЫВШИЕ НА СЕВЕР ЭТАПЫ ЗЭКОВ ИЗ-ЗА ОТСУТСТВИЯ БАРАКОВ
В МОРОЗЫ 40-50° ЗАГОНЯЛИ НА НОЧЬ В ЯМЫ, А ДНЕМ ОНИ СТРОИЛИ ДЛЯ
СЕБЯ НОВЫЙ ИТЛ. ИЗ ТЫСЯЧИ „ВРАГОВ НАРОДА" И „КУЛАКОВ" В ТАКИХ
УСЛОВИЯХ ДО ТЕПЛА ВЫЖИВАЛО НЕ БОЛЕЕ 250 ЧЕЛОВЕК...

'Enemies of the people' were kept in deep pits.

Often, convicts who had just arrived in the north were kept in pits for the night, because there were not enough barracks available. The temperature outside was 40° to 50° C below freezing. During the day, they built new ITL* barracks for themselves. In these conditions, out of every thousand 'enemies of the people' and *kulaks*,†
no more than two hundred and fifty survived to see the warmer seasons.‡

* ITL: *Ispravitelno-Trudovoi Lager* – literally 'Corrective Labour Camp'.
† A *kulak* (literally 'fist' in Russian) was a peasant wealthy enough to own a farm and hire labour. The *kulaks* tried to resist Stalin's collectivization. Many were arrested, exiled, or killed.
‡ 'In the early thirties labour camps spread over the territory of the USSR, especially the arctic regions. The prisoners built railways, roads, industrial complexes and cities around them; they manned the construction works and coal, lead, and gold mines, as well as the development of whole regions, like the gold-rich frigid Kolyma. The worst lot was that of forced-labour pioneers sent to set up brand new camps and work sites: they did not even have minimal accommodations until they had built them themselves. The mortality rate on such new projects was much higher than in veteran camp sites.' Leona Toker, *Return from the Archipelago*, 2000.

ЖЕНАМ, СЁСТРАМ И ДОЧЕРЯМ „ВРАГОВ НАРОДА"В ГУЛАГЕ ПРИ НЕ ВЫПОЛНЕНИИ НОРМЫ УБАВЛЯЛИ ПАЁК...

А НУ, СУЧКИ, ВСЕ ПО МЕСТАМ! ПУСТЬ ПОДЫХАЕТ, САМА ВИНОВАТА! (В ГУЛАГЕ НИКАКОЙ ТЕХНИКИ БЕЗОПАСНОСТИ НЕ БЫЛО И ВПОМИНЕ. ПРИ УВЕЧЬЕ В ТАЙГЕ, НА ШАХТАХ И ДРУГИХ РАБОТАХ ЗЭКАМ НЕ ОКА-ЗЫВАЛОСЬ ПОЧТИ НИКАКОЙ МЕДПОМОЩИ. СПИСАТЬ ТЕЛОГРЕЙКУ ИЛИ ОБУВЬ БЫЛО ВОЛОКИТНЕЕ,ЧЕМ УМЕРШЕГО ИЛИ УБИТОГО ЗЭКА...)

In the Gulag, if the wives, sisters and daughters of the 'enemies of the people' did not meet their daily quotas, their rations were curtailed.

'Back to work, bitches! Let her lie there and die. It's her own fault.'

There was no workplace safety to speak of in the Gulag. If a prisoner was injured in the taiga, at the mines, or other workplaces, almost no medical care was provided. It was easier to account for a prisoner who had died of 'natural causes' or injuries, than it was to account for an item of clothing (such as a jacket) or footwear.

„ПОВТОРНИКИ" — БЕСПРАВНЫЕ РАБЫ УРОДЛИВОЙ, ЗВЕРСКОЙ КАТОРЖНОЙ СИСТЕМЫ „СТАЛИНСКОГО ФАШИЗМА" В СССР...

С 1946 по 1953 годы в ОПЕРЧАСТИ („ХИТРЫЙ ДОМИК", „КУМОВСКАЯ") ИТЛ ГУЛАГА ВЫЗЫВАЛИСЬ „ВРАГИ НАРОДА", ОСУЖДЕННЫЕ ПО СТ. 58 УК РСФСР В 1936-1940 ГОДАХ, ДЛЯ ОЗНАКОМЛЕНИЯ И ЛИЧНОЙ РОСПИСИ В БЛАНКАХ ОБ АВТОМАТИЧЕСКОМ ПРОДЛЕНИИ СРОКА ЗАКЛЮЧЕНИЯ НА 5 ЛЕТ БЕЗ СУДА. ТАК ПОЯВИЛИСЬ МИЛЛИОНЫ ЗЭКОВ — „ПОВТОРНИКОВ"...

_Povtorniks_* were the slaves of the ugly, bestial system of hard labour of 'Stalin's Fascism' in the USSR.

During the period 1946 to 1953, the 'enemies of the people' who had been sentenced under Article 58[†] (of the Penal Code of the Russian SFSR) between 1936 and 1940, were called into the Operative Headquarters (the 'sneaky house' or 'favouritism room,' as it was also called) of the Gulag prisons. They were made to read and sign papers that automatically extended their sentence for five more years without trial. This practise created millions of _povtorniks_.

* _Povtorniks_ – taken from the word _povtor_, 'repeat' (the prison term).
[†] See page 81.

РАЗВОД ЗЭКОВ НА РАБОТУ,ГДЕ ДОЛЖНЫ „ПРИСУТСТВОВАТЬ" УМЕРШИЕ НОЧЬЮ
В БАРАКАХ И БОЛЬНЫЕ С ТЕМПЕРАТУРОЙ 38-39°... ПЛАН-ЛЮБОЙ ЦЕНОЙ...
-ОТРЯДЫ, СТРОЙСЯ! ВЗЯТЬСЯ ПОД РУКИ! ПРЕДУПРЕЖДАЮ,-ШАГ ВЛЕВО,ШАГ
ВПРАВО СЧИТАЮТСЯ ПОБЕГОМ,И КОНВОЙ ПРИМЕНЯЕТ ОРУЖИЕ БЕЗ ПРЕДУ-
ПРЕЖДЕНИЯ! ОРКЕСТР-МАРШ! ПЕРВАЯ ПЯТЕРКА-ВПЕРЕД! НАРЯДЧИК,КО МНЕ ..

Prisoner job assignment routine. Everybody must be 'present' during the roll call, including the prisoners who died in the barracks the previous night, and the sick with temperatures of 38° to 39° C. The government plan must be fulfilled at any price.

'Brigades, fall in! Link arms! If you make a step to the left or to the right, it will be considered an attempt to escape, and the guards will shoot to kill without warning. Band, begin to play! First five-man brigade, march! Assigner, approach me!'

501=Я СТРОЙКА *ГУЛАГА* МВД СССР. *ТРАМБО*
ДЕРЕВЯННЫМ КАТКОМ ИЗ ДОСОК, ПОЛАЯ ЧА

ЕГИПЕТСКУЮ ПИРАМИДУ ХЕОПСА ОТДЕЛЯЛО 2
ЛЕЗНОЙ ДОРОГИ В СЕВЕРНОЙ ТУНДРЕ, НО МЕТО
МИ – РАБСКИЙ ПОДНЕВОЛЬНЫЙ ТРУД, УНЕСШ

Construction site No. 501 of the Gulag of the MVD of the USSR. Prisoners ramming soil for laying down rails and ties with a roller made from wooden boards. The hollow part of the roller is filled with rocks to increase its weight.

The Egyptian Cheops pyramid and Stalin's absurd 'railroad of death'* in the northern tundra are over two thousand years apart. But the methods and techniques of construction remained the same: slave labour that cost the lives of tens of thousands of the 'enemies of the people'.

АМИ ГРУНТА ДЛЯ УКЛАДКИ РЕЛЬСОВ И ШПАЛ
РОГО НАПОЛНЯЛАСЬ ДЛЯ ВЕСА КАМНЯМИ...

ОТ СТАЛИНСКОЙ АБСУРДНОЙ „МЁРТВОЙ" ЖЕ-
ОСОБЫ СТРОИТЕЛЬСТВА БЫЛИ ОДИНАКОВЫ-
ТКИ ТЫСЯЧ ЖИЗНЕЙ „ВРАГОВ НАРОДА"...

* In 1949 work began on the Salekhard to Igarka railway line, which was intended to provide a strategic link across northern Siberia. Known as the '501 Railroad' or the 'Road of Death', it was built entirely using Gulag labour. The mortality rate was high and every year the camps were resupplied with between 5,000 and 7,000 new workers. Harsh conditions: permafrost and temperatures of 60° C below freezing in winter; boggy marsh, disease, mosquitoes and horseflies in summer; hampered the construction. Following Stalin's death in 1953 the project was abandoned with only 434 of the planned 806 miles completed. It has since fallen into complete disrepair.

Re-education

ЧТЕНИЕ СОЦОБЯЗАТЕЛЬСТВА В ИТЛ ГУЛАГА. ЭТО ОДИН ИЗ МНОГИХ АБСУРДОВ КОММУНИСТИЧЕСКОЙ ИДЕОЛОГИИ – СОЦИАЛИСТИЧЕСКОЕ СОРЕВНОВАНИЕ МЕЖДУ БРИГАДАМИ И ОТРЯДАМИ ВОРОВ, ГРАБИТЕЛЕЙ, НАСИЛЬНИКОВ И УБИЙЦ...

Writing on the placard: **'Only through honest labour will you gain the right to be paroled'**. The paper in the hands of the guard reads: **'Socialist Self-Obligations'**.[*]

The announcement of socialist self-obligations in the Gulag prison camp. This is one of the many absurd aspects of the Communist ideology – a socialist competition[†] between the workers' brigades composed of thieves, robbers, rapists and murderers.

* 'Socialist self-obligations' were voluntary, but in reality they were expected of the workforce. The results of these declarations were supposed to exceed the production plan set by the government.
† 'Socialist competition' was encouraged between state enterprises and was also common between individuals within enterprises. Teams of workers competed against each other to produce more goods, transport more people, save more resources, etc., with prizes awarded to the winners. However, the formalism that reigned over the country meant that the results were either falsified or judged on quantity rather than quality.

ПОЛИТЗАНЯТИЯ С УГОЛОВНИКАМИ В *ИТЛ ГУЛАГА МВД СССР*...
– ЗАКЛЮЧЕННЫЙ *ИВАНОВ*, РАССКАЖИТЕ ПО ТЕМЕ ПРОШЛЫХ ЗАНЯТИЙ
ОБ *АПРЕЛЬСКИХ ТЕЗИСАХ* – ПРОГРАММЕ *ОКТЯБРЬСКОЙ РЕВОЛЮЦИИ*...
– Я ЧТО-ТО ПЛОХО ПОМНЮ, ГРАЖДАНИН НАЧАЛЬНИК... А ЭТО, КАЖЕТСЯ,
О ТОМ ЛЫСЕНЬКОМ, КАРТАВЕНЬКОМ, КОТОРЫЙ В *ПИТЕРЕ* НА БАНУ
ЧТО-ТО С БРОНЕВИЧКА ХРЮКНУЛ?...

Political Information classes in the Gulag prison camp.

'Prisoner Ivanov, tell us again what you learned in the previous lesson about the April Theses[*] – the programme of the October Revolution.'

'I'm not sure I remember it right, chief. Was it about that bald guy with a burr[†] that shouted out something from an armoured vehicle at the train station in Leningrad?'[‡]

[*] The April Theses were a series of directives by Vladimir Lenin given to the Bolsheviks when he returned to Petrograd from his exile in Switzerland on the night of 16th April 1917. (They were originally rejected by the Bolsheviks.) The full theses text was later published in the newspaper *Pravda*.

[†] The prisoner is making a reference to Lenin's speech impediment.

[‡] Baldaev is making a statement about the impossibility of re-educating criminal inmates (the tattooed hands show that this inmate is a criminal rather than a political prisoner). The authorities believed that it was not worth trying to re-educate the 'socially dangerous' political prisoners, instead concentrating their efforts on the 'socially close' thieves-in-law: 'A 1940 NKVD directive on the cultural-educational work of the camps stated explicitly that those who had committed counter-revolutionary crimes were not suitable targets for re-education. In camp theatrical productions, they were allowed to play musical instruments, but not to speak or sing.' Anne Applebaum, *Gulag: A History*, 2003.

РАЗГОВОР ЗЭКОВ О „СОЦЗАКОННОСТИ"В СОВЕТСКОМ СОЮЗЕ...

СССР- САМОЕ ДЕМОКРАТИЧЕСКОЕ И ПРАВОВОЕ ГОСУДАРСТВО ВО ВСЕМ МИРЕ

-ГРАЖДАНИН ПРОКУРОР, ВОТ МНЕ ДАЛИ 5 ЛЕТ ЗА 3 МЕШКА КОМБИКОР-
МОВ, КОТОРЫХ НЕТ В ПРОДАЖЕ, А Я ХОТЕЛ ВЫРАСТИТЬ ПОРОСЁНКА, А ЭТА
ПАРТИЙНАЯ МАФИЯ ИЗ КПСС ВОРУЕТ МИЛЛИОНАМИ, БЕРЁТ ВЗЯТКИ И
ОТ ЭТОГО „НЕДУГА" ЛЕЧИТСЯ В САНАТОРИЯХ И НЕ СИДИТ, КАК Я, В ЛАГЕРЕ...

A conversation about 'social justice' in the Soviet Union...
The placard on the wall reads: **'The USSR is the Most Democratic Country in the World, where the Rule of Law Reigns'.**[*]

'Comrade Public Prosecutor, I was given five years in prison for stealing three bags of mixed fodder. You can't buy it in a store and I had a pig to feed. Now, this mob in the Communist Party steals millions, takes bribes, and is treated for this "illness" in resorts and sanatoriums. And unlike me, it doesn't do time in the camps.'

* A political slogan from the Gorbachev era.

ОДИН ИЗ ВИДОВ ПРОФИЛАКТИКИ В ИТЛ ГУЛАГА...

ДЛЯ УСТРАШЕНИЯ ЗЭКОВ С ЦЕЛЬЮ УКРЕПЛЕНИЯ ДИСЦИПЛИНЫ И ПОДНЯТИЯ ПРОИЗВОДИТЕЛЬНОСТИ РАБСКОГО ТРУДА, У КПП ИТЛ ГУЛАГА КЛАЛИ РАССТРЕЛЯННЫХ ПО ПРИГОВОРУ ЛАГЕРНОЙ ТРОЙКИ. КОНВОЙ ПРОВОДИЛ БРИГАДЫ „ВРАГОВ НАРОДА" ИЗ ЗОНЫ НА РАБОТЫ МИМО ЭТИХ ТРУПОВ, КОТОРЫЕ НЕ УБИРАЛИСЬ ПО НЕСКОЛЬКО ДНЕЙ...

One kind of preventative measure in the Gulag.
The signs on the building read: **'Back to Freedom with a Clear Conscience!'**; **'Long Live the VKP(b)!*'**; **'Checkpoint No.3'**. The signs on the dead bodies read: **'For breaching internal prison regulations'**; **'For attempted prison revolt'**; **'For the refusal to w[ork]'**.

To deter prisoners, strengthen discipline and increase the output of slave labour, the bodies of prisoners executed by the *troika*[†] were laid down in rows by a checkpoint. The guards led the units of the 'enemies of the people' past the corpses when the prisoners marched to and from work. The corpses were not removed for days.

* See page 19.
[†] The NKVD *Troikas* (triumvirate), consisted of three people: the Head of the local NKVD subdivision, the Secretary of the Regional Committee and the Public Prosecutor. They were were used as an instrument of extrajudicial punishment against anti-Soviet elements between 1937 and 1938.

Children

Будни ГУЛАГА „ДА ЗДРАВСТВУЕТ СОЦИАЛИС

В ЖЕНСКОМ ЛАГЕРЕ „МАМОЧЕК" ДЕТИ ЗЭЧЕК „ВРАГОВ НАРОДА,"И УГОЛОВНИЦ СОДЕРЖАЛИСЬ ВМ
ПИТАНИЯ РОСЛИ РАХИТИЧНЫМИ ЗАМОРЫШАМИ С ПОЗДНИМ РАЗВИТИЕМ, ЗАТЕМ ДЕТИ ОТБИР
ПОСЛЕ РЕКВИЗИЦИИ ДЕТЕЙ РЫДАЛИ, ТЕРЯЛИ СОН, ВСЯКИЙ ИНТЕРЕС К ЖИЗНИ, ПОПАДАЛ.

**The Daily Life of the Gulag. 'Long Live the Socialist Gulag – A Big Step Toward Communism!' Minister of
Internal Affairs, L.P. Beria.**

In a women's prison camp for 'mummies', the children of both 'enemies of the people' and ordinary criminals,
were held together with their mothers until they were aged between two to five (at the discretion of the
administration). Because no children's food was available to them, they grew very weak – their growth was stunted,
and they suffered from rickets.* They were then taken away and put in special orphanages and technical
schools. After they were deprived of their children many inmate mothers, slaves of the Gulag camps, sobbed
continually, developed insomnia and lost interest in living. They ended up in prison psychiatric institutions.

ГУЛАГ–БОЛЬШОЙ ШАГ В КОММУНИЗМ!" *Министр МВД Л.П.Берия*

' ДО 2-5 ЛЕТ (ВСЕ ЗАВИСЕЛО ОТ ПРОИЗВОЛА АДМИНИСТРАЦИИ). ИЗ-ЗА ОТСУТСТВИЯ ДЕТСКОГО
1СЬ В СПЕЦИАЛЬНЫЕ ДЕТСКИЕ ДОМА И ПТУ. МНОГИЕ ЗЭЧКИ-МАТЕРИ, РЯБЫНИ ИТЛ-ИТК ГУЛЯГА,
ХИАТРИЧЕСКИЕ БОЛЬНИЦЫ/

* 'I saw the nurses getting the children up in the mornings. They would force them out of their cold beds with shoves and kicks… pushing the children with their fists and swearing at them roughly, they took off their night-clothes and washed them in ice-cold water. The babies didn't even dare cry. They made little sniffing noises like old men and let out low hoots. This awful hooting noise would come from the cots for days at a time. Children already old enough to be sitting up or crawling would lie on their backs, their knees pressed to their stomachs, making these strange noises, like the muffled cooing of pigeons… Little Eleonora, who was now fifteen months old… stopped reaching out for me when I visited her; she would turn away in silence. On the last day of her life, when I picked her up (they allowed me to breast-feed her) she stared wide-eyed somewhere off into the distance, then started to beat her weak little fists on my face, clawing at my breast and biting it. Then she pointed down at her bed. In the evening when I came back with my bundle of firewood, her cot was empty. I found her lying naked in the morgue among the corpses of the adult prisoners.' Hava Volovich, *Till My Tale Is Told: Women's Memoirs of the Gulag*, 2001, (edited by Simeon Vilensky).

НАСИЛЬСТВЕННАЯ РЕКВИЗИЦИЯ ДЕТЕЙ, ЛАГЕРНЫХ ЗАМОРЫШЕЙ,-
„СТАЛИНСКИХ ВНУКОВ-ЗЭЧКОВ" У ЖЕНЩИН-ЗАКЛЮЧЕННЫХ В ИТЛ
ГУЛАГА ДЛЯ „МАМОЧЕК", Т.К.„ЗЭЧКИ", ПО МНЕНИЮ НАЧАЛЬСТВА, ОТ-
ВЛЕКАЮТ МАТЕРЕЙ ОТ ВЫПОЛНЕНИЯ ТРУДОВЫХ НОРМ И ЗАДАНИЯ
ГОСПЛАНА СССР ДЛЯ МВД...

Forced requisition of prisoners' sickly children, 'Stalin's grandchildren-inmates', as they were often called, from their imprisoned mothers in the Gulag prison camp for 'mummies'. The authorities believed that children distracted their mothers from meeting the labour quotas and prevented them from fulfilling the tasks of the Gosplan* of the USSR for the MVD.

* Gosplan – the State Committee for Planning, was established in 1921 to direct economic recovery. Its main task was to draw up the Five Year Plans to enable the rapid industrialisation of the Soviet Union.

9 ГРАММ- ПУТЕВКА КПСС В „СЧАСТЛИВОЕ ДЕТСТВО"

В СВЯЗИ С ПЕРЕПОЛНЕНИЕМ ДЕТСКИХ ДОМОВ ЧСИР В 1938-39 ГГ.
ДЕТИ „ВРАГОВ НАРОДА", „ПУСКАЛИСЬ В РАСХОД" В ГОРОДАХ:
ТОМСКЕ, МАРИИНСКЕ И СТ. ШИМАНОВСКОЙ В ЦИЗО „БАМЛАГА,"
Т. К. СЧИТАЛОСЬ, С ДОСТИЖЕНИЕМ СОВЕРШЕННОЛЕТИЯ, ОНИ
БУДУТ ОПАСНЫМИ ДЛЯ СУЩЕСТВУЮЩЕЙ СИСТЕМЫ ВЛАСТИ.

Nine grammes* – a ticket to a 'happy childhood', courtesy of the Communist Party.

Because the orphanages for the Family Members of Traitors of the Motherland were full, in 1938 and 1939 the children of the 'enemies of the people' were killed in Tomsk, Mariinsk and Shimanovskaya train station in the TzIZO[†] BAMLag[‡] isolation cell. It was thought that upon coming of age, they would pose a serious threat to the existing authorities.

* Nine grammes – the weight of a bullet.
[†] TzIZO – *Tzekh Ispolzovanniya Zavodskikh Otkhodov*: Recycling and Waste Disposal Facility.
[‡] BAMLag – the official abbreviation for the subdivision of the Gulag dealing with the construction of the Baikal-Amur Mainline railway during the period 1932 to 1948.

Hunger

– ЭЙ! ШАКАЛЫ, ФИЛОНЫ, ДОХОДЯГИ-ЖРАТЬ ПОДАНО!... ОБЕЗУМЕВШИЕ ОТ ГОЛОДА СЛАБОВОЛЬНЫЕ ЗЭКИ
НАХОДИЛИ „ПИТАНИЕ"НА ПОМОЙКЕ... КОММУНИСТАМ ТАК И НЕ УДАЛОСЬ „РАСЧЕЛОВЕЧИТЬ" В ГУЛАГЕ
СВЯЩЕННИКОВ, БЫВШИХ ДВОРЯН, ЦАРСКИХ ОФИЦЕРОВ, ЧИНОВНИКОВ, А ТАКЖЕ ИСТИННЫХ ВЫСОКОКУЛЬ-
ТУРНЫХ ИНТЕЛЛИГЕНТОВ, РАБОЧИХ И КРЕСТЬЯН С СИЛЬНОЙ ВОЛЕЙ И ГЛУБОКО ВЕРУЮЩИХ В БОГА...

Sign on the building reads: **'Canteen'**.

'Hey, jackals, slackers and goners!* Dinner is served.'
Weak-willed prisoners, mad from hunger, ate rubbish. But Communists in the Gulag never managed to
dehumanise priests, the former nobility, czarist officers, officials and functionaries, the truly cultured
intelligentsia and strong-willed, pious workers and peasants.

* Those prisoners on the verge of death through starvation were referred to as *dokhodyagi* – 'goners'. Emaciated, apathetic and
exhausted, they would desperately search for and greedily consume any scrap of food. The camp system that caused their acute hunger
delt with them ruthlessly – as they grew weaker they were unable to meet the working norm, and their ration was reduced accordingly.
'The word *dokhodyaga* [goner], is derived from the verb *dokhodit* which means to arrive or reach... At first I could not see the
connection, but it was explained to me: the *dokhodyagi* were *'arrivists'*, those who had arrived at socialism, were the finished type of
citizen in the socialist society.' Vladimir Petrov, *It Happens In Russia: Seven Years Forced Labour in the Siberian Goldfields*, 1951.

ЧТО ЗНАЧИТ ДЛЯ ЧЕЛОВЕКА,КОТОРЫЙ РАБОТАЛ НА МОРОЗЕ ВЕСЬ ДЕНЬ, МИСКА ПОХЛЁБКИ И ПАЙКА ХЛЕБА 300 ГРАММ? ПЫТАЯСЬ ОБМАНУТЬ И УСПОКОИТЬ ГОЛОДНЫЙ ЖЕЛУДОК,ЗЭКИ ВАРИЛИ ПАЙКУ В СОЛЁНОЙ ВОДЕ,И КАК РЕЗУЛЬТАТ-ОПУХАНИЕ,БИРКА НА НОГЕ И КЛАДБИЩЕ ИТЛ... ПО СЛОВАМ УЗНИКОВ,В ГУЛАГЕ БЫЛО ХУЖЕ,ЧЕМ В ЛАГЕРЯХ А.ГИТЛЕРА.

Text on the banner reads: **'Forward, to Communism!'**; text on the bulletin board reads: **'Fire Safety Rules of the Prison Camp'**. The graffiti reads (top to bottom): **'Death to Coppers!'**; **'S.O.S.'**; **'Hello to Goners from the Next World'**; **'White Swan'**; **'Perm to Cons'**.

What is a bowl of soup and 300 grams of bread to a man who has worked in frigid temperatures all day? To deceive and calm their empty stomachs, prisoners boiled their rationed bread in salted water. The result? Swelling, a tag on the foot and then the prison graveyard… According to its prisoners, the Gulag was worse than Hitler's concentration camps.[*]

[*] 'In one cell the cons had… got hold of a razor blade somewhere and for several days had collected up paper. When everything was ready they each cut a piece of flesh from their bodies – some from the stomach, others from the leg. Everybody's blood was collected into one bowl, the flesh was thrown in, a small fire was made from the paper and some books and then they started to half-fry, half-stew their feast. When the wardens noticed that something was wrong and burst into the cell the stew was still not cooked and the cons, falling over themselves and burning their fingers, grabbed the pieces from the bowl and stuffed them into their mouths.' Anatoly Marchenko, *My Testimony*, 1969.

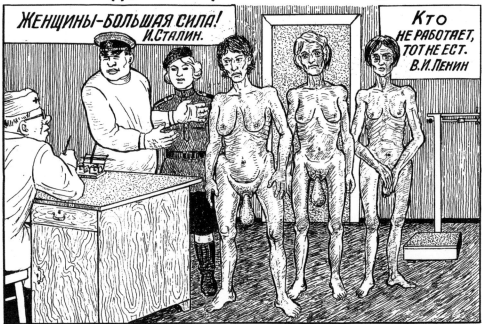

ЖЕНЫ, СЕСТРЫ И ДОЧЕРИ „ВРАГОВ НАРОДА" В ИТЛ ГУЛАГА НКВД „СОЛОВЕЦКОЙ ВЛАСТИ"НА МЕДОСМОТРЕ...

ЖЕНЩИНЫ—БОЛЬШАЯ СИЛА!
И.СТАЛИН.

КТО НЕ РАБОТАЕТ, ТОТ НЕ ЕСТ. В.И.ЛЕНИН

—ДОКТОР, ЭТИ ЗЭЧКИ ПЛАН НЕ ВЫПОЛНЯЮТ! ПОСАДИТЕ ИХ НА НУЛЁВКУ!...(В ИСПРАВИТЕЛЬНО-ТРУДОВЫХ ЛАГЕРЯХ (ИТЛ) ЖЕНЩИН „ВРАГОВ НАРОДА" ИСПОЛЬЗОВАЛИ НА САМЫХ ТЯЖЁЛЫХ РАБОТАХ—ЗЕМЛЯНЫХ И ЛЕСОПОВАЛЕ. В РЕЗУЛЬТАТЕ, ОТ ФИЗИЧЕСКОГО ПЕРЕНАПРЯЖЕНИЯ И НЕДОЕДАНИЯ, У МНОГИХ ЖЕНЩИН ПРОИСХОДИЛО ВЫПАДАНИЕ МАТКИ. БОЛЬНЫХ И СЛАБЫХ ЖЕНЩИН УМЕРЩВЛЯЛИ „НУЛЕВОЙ ДИЕТОЙ", Т.Е. ГОЛОДОМ..)

Wives, sisters, and daughters of the 'enemies of the people' undergoing a medical examination in the Corrective Labour Camp of the Gulag system, the 'Solovki Authorities'.
Sign on the left reads: **'Women are a great power! J. Stalin'**; sign on the right reads: **'He who does not work, neither shall he eat.* V. I. Lenin'.**

'Doctor, these cons didn't meet their labour quota. Prescribe them the VLCD!'
In corrective labour camps, female 'enemies of the people' were given the hardest jobs – digging the earth and lumbering. Many suffered from prolapse of the uterus from overstrain and starvation. Ailing and weak women were starved to death, which was referred to as 'going on the VLCD' (Very Low Calorie Diet).

* '... purge victims faced a lethal combination of chronic hunger, overwork and neglect. About half their calorie intake consisted of bread (on average, about a pound a day); the rest came from trash soup (*balanda*) cooked from calculated amounts of potatoes, groats, sugar and fats; sometimes they would also get a few spoonfuls of lean porridge. The portions of cooked foods were usually shrunk by theft; the bread rations were cut and the porridge denied if the prisoner did not meet the production quotas. Few could possibly meet the quotas since these were too high even for skilled, able-bodied labourers: as the prisoners got less food, they had even less strength to work and thus entered a "vicious spiral" (Ekart 1954).' Leona Toker, *Return from the Archipelago*, 2000.

The Power of the Criminals

—ТЫ, КОНТРА, ЗАТКНИ ХЛЕБАЛЬНИК! СБЛОЧИВАЙ ПАЛЬТУХАН, ПОЛУСАП-
ОЖКИ „РУМЫНКИ", ШАРФИШКУ И КОХФТУ! ОТКАЧАЛА СВОИ ПРАВА В УНИ-
СТЕРТЕ СВОИМ СТУДЕНТАМ НА КАФИДРЕ… ОГРАБЛЕНИЕ УГОЛОВНИ-
КАМИ ЗЭКОВ „ВРАГОВ НАРОДА" В ГУЛАГЕ, ОТБИРАНИЕ ПАЕК И ПОСЫЛ-
ОК БЫЛО ОБЫЧНЫМ

'Shut your mouth, counter-revolutionary! Take off your coat, boots, scarf and jacket. Rights-rubbish! You tell
that to your students in your university.'
Robbing 'enemies of the people' of their clothes, rations and parcels by criminals in the Gulag was commonplace.

— ДЕВКИ, МОЧИТЕ ЭТУ КОНТРУ-ЖИДОВКУ, ЧТОБЫ ХВОСТА НЕ ПОДНИМА-
ЛА!... ИЗБИЕНИЯ, САДИЗМ, УБИЙСТВА, ЗВЕРИНЫЙ РАСИСТСКИЙ АНТАГО-
НИЗМ В ГУЛАГЕ ДОСТИГЛИ ВСЕХ ВЕРШИН. ВОРОВКИ В ЗАКОНЕ „МА-
ХАНШИ"И ИХ ПОДРУЧНЫЕ „ЖУЧКИ" БЫЛИ ХОЗЯЙКАМИ В ЖЕНСКИХ ЛА-
ГЕРЯХ И НАХОДИЛИСЬ В ПРИВИЛЕГИРОВАННОМ ПОЛОЖЕНИИ...

Words on the bucket read: **'Barrack No.6. Brigade No.12'**.

'Girls! Beat up this yid counter-revolutionary, so she keeps her tail down!'

The Gulag witnessed the most extreme forms of beating, sadism, murder and savage racial antagonism. *Makhanshas* (female 'legitimate' thieves), and *zhuchkas* (their accomplices), were the highest, most privileged caste in women's prison camps.

НАПАДЕНИЕ УГОЛОВНИКОВ НА ЗЭКОВ ИНОСТРАНЦЕВ-
КОММУНИСТОВ, ПРИБЫВШИХ В СССР ПОМОЧЬ В СТРОИ-
ТЕЛЬСТВЕ СОЦИАЛИЗМА И ЗАТЕМ ПОПАВШИХ В ИТЛ
ГУЛАГА...

Criminals assaulting foreign Communist prisoners who had come to the USSR to help build socialism, and
were then imprisoned in Gulag camps.

По указке работников НКВД или ИТЛ ГУЛАГА уголовники совершали акты мужеложества над „врагами народа"...

– Говорят, на воле директором, большим бугром был, потом ссучился и стал врагом народа? Мы тебя за это педиком-машкой сделаем!...
(Для совершения насильственного мужеложества над „врагом народа" уголовники-урки" нападали на жертву в жилой зоне ночью группой, при сопротивлении набрасывали петлю-удавку, вязали руки...)

By orders from the NKVD or Gulag prison authorities, criminals performed acts of sodomy on the 'enemies of the people'.

'They say you were some executive, some big shot out there, and then you became an enemy of the people? Well, now you're gonna be our bitch, you queer!'
(To forcibly sodomise an 'enemy of the people', *urkas* – criminal prisoners – attacked their victim in the barracks at night. If the victim tried to put up a fight, they put a stranglehold on him, tied up his hands, etc.)

УТОПЛЕНИЕ УГОЛОВНИКАМИ „ВРАГА НАРОДА" ПО НЕГЛАС-
НОМУ УКАЗАНИЮ НАЧАЛЬСТВА ИТЛ ГУЛАГА ДЛЯ УСТРА-
ШЕНИЯ ДРУГИХ ЗЭКОВ В БОЧКЕ С НЕЧИСТОТАМИ, КУДА
СЛИВАЕТСЯ СОДЕРЖИМОЕ ПАРАШ В ЗИМНЕЕ ВРЕМЯ...

Criminals drowning an 'enemy of the people' in a barrel of sewage waste (into which the toilets were emptied in the winter), by an unofficial order of the Gulag authorities. This was done to intimidate and plant fear into other prisoners.

„ЗАПЕЧАТАТЬ В БЕТОН"- СБРОС И УТОПЛЕНИЕ ЗЭКА-РАБОТЯГИ
ВОРАМИ В ЖИДКОМ, НЕ ЗАСТЫВШЕМ БЕТОНЕ ПРИ СТРОИТЕЛЬ-
СТВЕ ГИДРОЭЛЕКТРОСТАНЦИИ... СКОЛЬКО ТАКИХ ЖЕРТВ   В
БЕТОНЕ ГЭС, НЕ ИЗВЕСТНО...

'Sealing in concrete.' A worker prisoner is drowned in liquid concrete by criminal inmates during the construction of a hydroelectric power plant. There is no way of knowing how many victims the concrete structures of power plants hold.

„ЗАДЕЛАТЬ ТУРКА"-ПОСАДКА „ВРАГА НАРОДА" ЗА СОПРОТИВ-
ЛЕНИЕ ИЗДЕВАТЕЛЬСТВУ НА КОЛ ПО РЕШЕНИЮ „ВОРОВ В
ЗАКОНЕ" И МОЛЧАЛИВОГО ОДОБРЕНИЯ НАЧАЛЬСТВА ИТЛ...

'To pull a Turk',* impaling the 'enemy of the people' on a spike for resisting torture. The sentence is carried out by order of 'legitimate thieves' and with the silent approval of the authorities of the prison camp.

* Or: *zadelat turetsky shashlyk* – to make a Turkish kebab.

ВЫНОС ЗЭКА, ПРОИГРАВШЕГО СВОЮ ЖИЗНЬ В КАРТЫ, НА МОРОЗ...
–ОКРОПИ ЕГО СВЯТОЙ ВОДИЦЕЙ, ЧТОБЫ ЛУЧШЕ ЖИЛОСЬ НА ТОМ СВЕТЕ, А Я ЕГО ПРИСЫПЛЮ СНЕЖКОМ, ЧТОБЫ ВЕРТУХАИ СКОРО НЕ НАКНАЦАЛИ...

A prisoner, who has lost at cards,* is taken outside into the cold.

'Sprinkle some holy water on him, so he lives a better life in the next world. I'll cover him with snow so the guards don't spot him.'

* Games of cards were taken extremely seriously by criminals who viewed them as a way of demonstrating their cunning and bravado. They would often bet, and regularly lose, all their possessions. But games would not end there. Other inmates' belongings would be wagered, leading to beatings and even murders if the original owner of the 'lost' item refused to hand it over. Other punishments for failure to pay a debt included forcible tattooing (generally these 'shaming' tattoos depicted erotic scenes, in reality their purpose was far from erotic – to 'lower' the wearer's status within the criminal hierarchy), the cutting off of a 'twig' (a finger or toe), a 'dumpling' (ear), or the cutting out of a 'headlamp' (eye), and ultimately death (see pages 211-212).

„ЗАТКНУТЬ ХАЙЛО"– НАКАЗАНИЕ „ВРАГА НАРОДА" ЗА ТО, ЧТО ЧАСТО „ГРУБИЛ" НАЧАЛЬСТВУ ЛАГЕРЯ И ВТОРОЙ ТЕНЕ- ВОЙ ВЛАСТИ ИТЛ-ЛАГЕРНЫМ ПАХАНАМ („ВОРАМ В ЗАКОНЕ")

'To plug the throat', a punishment of an 'enemy of the people' for 'disrespect' toward the prison authorities and the second shadow power in the camp – the *pakhans** ('thieves in law': legitimate, authoritative thieves).

* These legitimate criminals distinguished themselves with their copious tattoos, displaying their history and status. In this drawing the criminal holding the hammer has the word *MIR* tattooed on his hand; an acronym that spells the Russian word for 'peace', but which stands for 'Shooting will reform me'. Baldaev exhaustively documented this secret code during his lifetime as a prison guard (see: Danzig Baldaev, *Russian Criminal Tattoo Encyclopaedia Volume I, II, III*, 2003-2008).

„ИНДИЙСКИЙ КРАНТ"-КАЗНЬ ЛУЧКОВОЙ ПИЛОЙ ПО РЕШЕ-
НИЮ ВОРОВСКОЙ СХОДКИ ИТЛ ГУЛАГА „ССУЧИВШЕГОСЯ"
УГОЛОВНИКА (ОТСТУПНИКА „ВОРОВСКОГО ЗАКОНА"И „ПРА-
ВИЛ")НА ДРОВЯНЫХ КОЗЛАХ ХОЗЯЙСТВЕННОГО ДВОРА...

'The Indian Krant',* the execution of a criminal who became a traitor, a *suka*,† to the 'thieves' law' by means of a hacksaw on the sawhorse in the utilities yards. The criminal was 'sentenced'‡ by a council of criminal 'authorities' in the Gulag.

* From *kranty* – finished, done in.

† *suka* – 'bitch', a criminal who had sided with the authorities to escape the rigours of the camp (see page 82).

‡ 'Sashka got up from his bunk. He was a young lad, bony, with hollow cheeks and watery blue eyes. Like all of us, his head was shaven. At twenty-three he had been jailed several times, and now, as a habitual criminal he had been sent to work in the mines of Kolyma. In the Arctic camps, Sashka, like all of those of his kind, refused to work and managed to live from what he stole from the kitchen or from the poor meals of his fellow inmates. He didn't earn much as he had to share the "fats" and the sugar with the senior thieves. Now he faced judgment for the worst offence in the criminal world: "selling" his brother thieves to the camp administration. For such a crime of betrayal there was only one punishment – death.' Michael Solomon, *Magadan*, 1971.

ПЕВЕЦ *ГУЛАГА* М.ГОРЬКИЙ УТВЕРЖДАЛ, ЧТО ЖАЛОСТЬ УНИЖАЕТ ЧЕЛОВЕКА. КОММУНИСТЫ И УГОЛОВНИКИ, КАК БЫ ПОДТВЕРЖДАЯ ЭТОТ ТЕЗИС, ЗВЕРСКИ И МЕТОДИЧНО УНИЧТОЖАЛИ ЛЮДЕЙ В ЗАСТЕНКАХ ВЧК-ГПУ-НКВД И *ГУЛАГЕ.* ОДНИМ ИЗ РАЗВЛЕЧЕНИЙ УГОЛОВНИКОВ В *ГУЛАГЕ* БЫЛО ИЗДЕВАТЕЛЬСТВО НАД ЗЭКАМИ С ПРИМЕНЕНИЕМ РАСКАЛЁННОГО НА ОГНЕ ЛОМА...

The bard of the Gulag,[*] Maxim Gorky, argued that pity humiliated man. Communists and criminals, as though trying to prove this idea, methodically and brutally exterminated people in the VChK-GPU-NKVD and the Gulag. Torture using a red hot crowbar was one of the favourite pastimes of criminal prisoners in the Gulag.

[*] This ironic title refers to the 1929 visit by Gorky to the Solovki Special Prison Camp (see page 15). Despite the authorities attempts to remove its more disturbing sights, he still witnessed the camp's harsh reality. He claimed his positive report, which described the system as 'indispensable', was a result of censorship. His real impressions remain disputed. In 1933-34 he edited *The White Sea-Baltic Canal*, a document that extolled the virtues of Gulag labour. 'Gorky's pronouncements, around now, are unrecognisable. He speaks the dialect of the regime in a tone of icy triumphalism.' Martin Amis, *Koba the Dread*, 2002.

„РАСКРОЙ ЧЕРЕПУШКИ,„ВРАГУ НАРОДА" ЗА ТО, ЧТО НЕ ДАВАЛ СОГЛАСИЯ УГОЛОВНИКАМ СПИСЫВАТЬ НА НИХ СВОИ ДНЕВНЫЕ ПРОЦЕНТЫ ВЫРАБОТКИ.

'Splitting open the skull of an enemy of the people', in revenge for his refusal to let the criminals appropriate his daily work quota.[*]

[*] Authoritative convicts made their minions write off their work quotas in their favour, or 'appropriated' them. This was a commonplace form of 'forced bribery'.

ИСПОЛНЕНИЕ „ПРИГОВОРА ПО РЕШЕНИЮ ВОРОВСКО-ГО СУДА" В ИСПРАВИТЕЛЬНО-ТРУДОВОМ ЛАГЕРЕ...

В УСЛОВИЯХ СТАЛИНСКИХ ЛАГЕРЕЙ ГУЛАГА ПРИ ПОПУСТИТЕЛЬСТВЕ АДМИНИСТРАЦИИ БЛАТАРИ-УГОЛОВНИКИ СОВЕРШАЛИ УБИЙСТВА ЗЭКОВ: ЭЛЕКТРОТОКОМ, НОЖАМИ, НА ВИСЕЛИЦЕ, ОТРУБАЛИ ГОЛОВЫ, РАСКАЛЁННЫЙ НА ОГНЕ ЛОМ ВТАЛКИВАЛИ В ЗАДНИЙ ПРОХОД И Т.Д. МНОГИЕ УГОЛОВНИКИ НА СВОЕМ СЧЕТУ ИМЕЛИ ПО 10 „БАРАНОВ" И БОЛЕЕ, Т.Е. УБИТЫХ ЗЭКОВ, В ТОМ ЧИСЛЕ „ВРАГОВ НАРОДА"...

Carrying out a death sentence 'by order of the court of thieves' in a prison camp.
Writing on the wall: **'We Will Smash Capitalism!'**.

In Stalin's Gulag system 'privileged' criminals murdered other inmates with the collusion of the administration.[*] They electrocuted, stabbed, hanged and decapitated them, inserted red-hot crowbars into the anus, etc. Many criminals had ten or more 'sheep', i.e. murdered prisoners, including 'enemies of the people', on their conscience.

[*] 'Such killings were particularly common in the Gulag following the repeal of capital punishment for murder by a decree of 26th May 1947. This was a deliberate move to cut back the numbers of convicts. I saw and spoke with these killers in corrective labour camps in Tuluna, Angara and Irkutsk... They would kill the first convict they came across in order to get into prison, they had no desire to leave the camps – since there was no one waiting for them outside and they had grown used to imprisonment.' Danzig Baldaev, *Russian Criminal Tattoo Encyclopaedia Volume II*, 2006.

**ПРИВЕДЕНИЕ В ИСПОЛНЕНИЕ СМЕРТНОГО ПРИГОВОРА ВОРАМИ.
–ПУСТЬ ЗНАЮТ ЧУХНЫ-ВРАГИ РУССКИХ, ЧТО НАДО ОТДАВАТЬ ПО-
СЫЛКИ С ЭСТОНСКИМ САЛОМ И МЁДОМ „ВОРАМ В ЗАКОНЕ"...**

Graffiti on the walls reads: **'Kill Bitches!'**; **'Osipov is a cannibal and an old cock'**; **'Death to contras'**; **'Gunners'**; **'Brigade No.5'**; **'Death to coppers'**; **'Kum's a moron and an arsehole'**; **'Don't turn your head around when you sit down to take a shit'**; **'Death to Yids and prison guards'**; **'Death to slant-eyed riffraff'**; **'The supervisor of brigade No.12 is a moron and a thief'**; **'Prosecutor Ivlev is an arsehole'**.

Thieves carrying out a death sentence.*

'That'll teach them riffraff, Russian-haters, to give parcels with Estonian ham and honey to legitimate thieves.'

* 'In one incident in 1951, a thieves' court sentenced a thief called Yurilkin to death. Camp authorities heard of the sentence, and transferred Yurilkin, first to another camp, then to a transit prison, then to a third camp in a completely different part of the country. Nevertheless, two thieves-in-law finally tracked him down there and murdered him – four years later. They were subsequently tried and executed for murder, but even such punishments were not necessarily a deterrent. In 1956, the Soviet prosecutor's office circulated a frustrated note complaining that "this criminal formation exists in all Corrective-Labour Camps, and often the decision of the group to murder one or another prisoner who is in a different camp is executed in that camp unquestioningly."' Anne Applebaum, *Gulag: A History*, 2003.

ЖЕНЩИН И ДЕВУШЕК, „ВРАГОВ НАРОДА," ВТАЛКИВАЛИ В КАМЕРЫ УГОЛОВНИКОВ НА ОДНУ НОЧЬ И БОЛЕЕ...

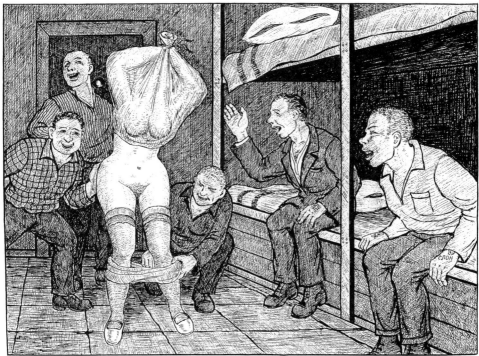

ЧТОБЫ ВЫРВАТЬ У ЖЕНЩИН И ДЕВУШЕК, „ВРАГОВ НАРОДА," НУЖНЫЕ СЛЕДОВАТЕЛЮ НКВД ПОКАЗАНИЯ (КРОМЕ ДОПРОСА 3-Й СТЕПЕНИ-ПЫТОК), ИХ ПОМЕЩАЛИ В КАМЕ-РЫ УГОЛОВНИКОВ, ГДЕ ОНИ ПОДВЕРГАЛИСЬ ЗВЕРСКОМУ ГЛУМЛЕНИЮ И ГРУППО-ВЫМ ИЗНАСИЛОВАНИЯМ, ПОСЛЕ ЧЕГО ЖЕРТВЫ ВПОСЛЕДСТВИИ ЧАСТО КОН-ЧАЛИ ЖИЗНЬ САМОУБИЙСТВОМ (ВЕШАЛИСЬ, РЕЗАЛИ ВЕНЫ, ЕЛИ ЗЕМЛЮ И Т.Д.)...

Female 'enemies of the people' were shoved into cells with criminals and locked there overnight or longer...

To make the women and girls who were 'enemies of the people' sign statements conjured up by an NKVD interrogator, in addition to undergoing third degree interrogation (torture) they were put in prison cells with criminals. There they were brutally gang-raped.* After this, the victims often committed suicide (hanged themselves, sliced their veins, swallowed dirt, etc.).

* Criminals treated women with contempt and 'rape in chorus' (group rape) was a common pastime. They considered prostitution a woman's legitimate work, often living from the profits – assuming all women would relish a life spent serving a professional criminal. Women were regarded as an exchangeable property; no emotional attachments were permitted toward them. A female thief would be expected to obey both the thieves' law and the 'property' law. A criminal's mother was the only woman who received their apparent respect, and whose honour was scrupulously defended. But this melodramatic adulation was a hollow affectation, an expression of prison sentimentality that helped paint the criminal as a romantic figure in Russian folklore.

Subjugation and Punishment

ЗАКЛЮЧЕННЫХ „ВРАГОВ НАРОДА" ЗА МАЛЕЙШИЕ „ВОЗРАЖЕНИЯ" В ИТЛ САЖАЛИ В ХОЛОДНЫЙ КАРЦЕР, ГДЕ СТЕНЫ БЫЛИ СЫРЫМИ ИЛИ ПРОМЕРЗШИМИ...

Graffiti on the walls reads: **'Vorkuga-Inta'**; **'Perm'**; **'Karalag'**; etc. (various geographic names where camps were located).

For the slightest 'objections', the 'enemies of the people' were put in a cold isolation cell. The walls of the cell were either damp or completely frozen.*

* The following description of an isolation cell relates to the experience of a poet. The conditions were documented in 1983, when she was serving a seven year sentence for anti-Soviet agitation and propaganda. 'The worst feature of the SHIZO [isolation cell] is the intense cold… The cell has a wooden floor with gaps between its boards, and underneath, a layer of solid cement, said to be about 40-50 centimetres thick. The window has bars but often no glass. In SHIZO prisoners receive food rations only on alternate days. On the "empty" day, they are given just bread and a hot drink three times. Light bedding is handed out to them at night and taken away again in the morning, so there is nothing they can use to keep warm.' Irina Ratushinskaya, *No, I'm Not Afraid*, 1986.

ЗА „ПРОВИННОСТЬ" ЗЭКОВ В СОЛОВЕЦКОМ ЛОН В ШИЗО НА ГОРЕ СЕКИРНОЙ В ХРАМЕ
ВОЗНЕСЕНИЯ ЗАСТАВЛЯЛИ „ВОЗНОСИТЬСЯ"—СИДЕТЬ ЧАСАМИ И СУТКАМИ НА
ЖЕРДОЧКАХ (ШЕСТЫ-НАСЕСТЫ).КТО ПАДАЛ ОТ УСТАЛОСТИ ИЛИ СНА, ПОДВЕРГАЛСЯ
„ВЕСЕЛЬЮ",Т.Е. ЗВЕРСКОМУ ИЗБИЕНИЮ И ОДЕВАНИЮ ПЕТЛИ НА ШЕЮ. ТАКИЕ
НАКАЗАНИЯ БЫЛИ И В „КОМАНДИРОВКАХ"—ДРУГИХ ОТДЕЛЕНИЯХ СЛОН ГПУ-НКВД

Banner on the wall reads: **'Death to the Counter-revolution!'**.

In the isolation cell of the Solovki Special Prison Camp, in the Church of the Resurrection,[*] prisoners who breached internal regulations were forcibly 'resurrected', i.e. they were forced to perch on beams for hours or even days. Those who fell off were 'tickled', that is they were severely beaten and a noose was put on their necks. Such punishments were also used in other camps of the Solovki prison.

[*] The prison was a converted 15th century monastery, its Church of the Resurrection was used by the authorities as an isolation cell.

НАКАЗАНИЕ ЗЭКА ЗА НАПАДЕНИЕ НА НАДЗИРАТЕЛЯ ОДЕВАНИЕМ НАРУЧНИКОВ – „КОРОМЫСЛОМ НАВЫВОРОТ"

ЗЭК „КОРОМЫСЛО НАВЫВОРОТ" ВЫДЕРЖИВАЕТ НЕ БОЛЕЕ 15-20 МИНУТ, С ПОДВЕСКОЙ НА КРЮК ИЛИ ВЕРЕВКЕ НЕ БОЛЕЕ 5-7МИНУТ И ПОВТОРНЫХ НАПАДЕНИЙ НА НАДЗОРСОСТАВ НЕ СОВЕРШАЕТ НИ В ТЮРЬМЕ, НИ В ИТЛ...

Punishing a convict for assaulting a guard by handcuffing him 'yoke backwards'.
Various graffiti on the walls reads: **'Zhorka is a stoolie'**; **'Death to coppers'**; **'Vaga was here'**; etc.

A prisoner 'yoked backwards' could only bear it for fifteen to twenty minutes. If additionally hung by a rope or a hook, no more than five to seven minutes. Following such punishment, he would never repeat the assault in prison or in the camp.

С ЦЕЛЬЮ УНИЖЕНИЯ ИНТЕЛЛИГЕНТА,„ВРАГА НАРОДА,“ СА-
ЖАЛИ НА ЦЕПЬ И ДАВАЛИ ГАЗЕТУ „ПРАВДА,“ А ТАКЖЕ ЗАСТАВ-
ЛЯЛИ ОПРАВЛЯТЬСЯ В ПОСУДУ, ИЗ КОТОРОЙ ОН ЕЛ БАЛАНДУ...

Sign on the wall reads: **'Under the wise guidance of the Party, the Soviet people will reach Communism – the pinnacle of human happiness!'**. The prisoner sits on the newspaper: ***Pravda***.

To demoralise and humiliate an intellectual 'enemy of the people', he was chained and given a copy of the *Pravda* newspaper. He was also forced to defecate in the same bowl he used to eat his *balanda* (prison soup of minimal nutritional value).

149

ОДИН ИЗ ВИДОВ НАКАЗАНИЯ ЗЭКОВ ЗА ОСЛУШАНИЕ—
„ГОЛОСОВАТЬ НА СОЛНЦЕ" ИЛИ
„ СУШИТЬ ЛАПКИ"...

– НАЧАЛЬНИК, ПРОСТИ! ХРИСТОМ БОГОМ ПРОШУ! РУКИ УСТАЛИ...
–ОПУСТИТ РУКИ, ПОЛОСНИ ОЧЕРЕДЬЮ! СПИШЕМ ЗА ПОПЫТКУ БЕЖАТЬ...
(„ГОЛОСОВАТЬ" СТАВИЛИ ИНОГДА „КРЕСТОМ," Т.Е. РУКИ В СТОРОНУ НА
УРОВНЕ ПЛЕЧ, ИЛИ НА ОДНОЙ НОГЕ „ЦАПЛЕЙ"-ПО ПРИХОТИ КОНВОЯ...)

Another type of punishment for disobedience was called 'Voting in the Sun' or 'Drying the Paws'.

'Forgive me, chief! For Christ's sake! My arms are tired.'
'If he puts them down, fire a few rounds at him. We'll write it off as an escape attempt.'
(Occasionally, prisoners were forced to 'Cross Vote', spreading out their arms and holding them at shoulder level, or stand on one leg in 'The Crane', depending on the inclination of the guards.)

Ложись! Встать! Ложись! Встать! Ложись!........
Я ВАС ВСЕХ НАУЧУ ЛЮБИТЬ ПОРЯДОК И СОВЕТСКУЮ ВЛАСТЬ!

ЭТО ОДИН ИЗ РАСПРОСТРАНЁННЫХ ВИДОВ ИСТЯЗАНИЯ ЗЭКОВ-
"ВРАГОВ НАРОДА" В ИСПРАВИТЕЛЬНО (ИСТРЕБИТЕЛЬНО)-ТРУ-
ДОВЫХ ЛАГЕРЯХ (ИТЛ) ГУЛАГА „КЛАСТЬ ЗА ПРОВИННОСТЬ"
ЛЮДЕЙ В СНЕГ, ГРЯЗЬ, ЛУЖИ, Т.К. ВСЁ ЗАВИСЕЛО ОТ ПОЛ-
НЕЙШЕГО ПРОИЗВОЛА АДМИНИСТРАЦИИ И ОХРАНЫ.
ЗА НЕПОВИНОВЕНИЕ ЗЭКИ РАССТРЕЛИВАЛИСЬ НА МЕСТЕ...

'Down! Up! Down! Up! Down!... I'll teach you all to love law and order, and Soviet power!

One of the more common forms of torture for 'enemies of the people' in the corrective (extermination) labour camps of the Gulag system – 'dropping down for misdemeanours'. People were forced to lie down on the snow, dirt, puddles, etc., depending on the whim of the administration and guards. Those who disobeyed were shot on the spot.

Вид истязания - „На перекачку"...

ЗАКЛЮЧЁННОГО ВЫВОДИЛИ ЗА ОХРАНЯЕМУЮ ЗОНУ И ЗАСТАВЛЯЛИ ПОД СТРАХОМ СМЕРТИ ЧЕРПАТЬ ВЕДРОМ ВОДУ ИЗ ОДНОЙ ПРОРУБИ(ЛУНКИ) И ВЫЛИВАТЬ В ДРУГУЮ ПРОРУБЬ, РАСПОЛОЖЕННУЮ В 15-20 МЕТРАХ ОТ ПЕРВОЙ. ПРИ „ДВОЙНОЙ ПЕРЕКАЧКЕ" ЧЕРПАЛИ ВЕДРОМ ВОДУ ИЗ ПРОРУБИ И СРАЗУ ВЫЛИВАЛИ В ЭТУ ЖЕ ПРОРУБЬ, ЗАЧЕРПНУВ ПОВТОРНО, НЕСЛИ ВОДУ В ВЕДРЕ И ВЫЛИВАЛИ В ДРУГУЮ ПРОРУБЬ..

'Pumping' – another form of torture.

The convict was taken outside the guarded zone and forced – under punishment of death – to draw water with a bucket from one hole in the ice and pour it out into another hole, fifteen to twenty metres away from the first. 'Double pumping' involved drawing water out of the first hole and pouring it immediately back into the same hole; then drawing water out again, and pouring it out into another hole.

ЗВЕРСКОЕ ПРАВИЛО –„БЕЗ ПОСЛЕДНЕГО!"
(ЗА 15 СЕКУНД ПЕРЕД „СОКРАЩЕНИЕМ"...)

– ПОЩАДИ, НАЧАЛЬНИК! ДОМА ОСТАЛИСЬ ТРОЕ ДЕТЕЙ, ЖЕНА, БОЛЬНАЯ МАТЬ...
– НЕ МОГУ – ПРИКАЗ НАЧАЛЬСТВА! ВЕЛЕНО ВРАГОВ НАРОДА НЕ ЩАДИТЬ!
(НЕКОТОРЫЕ НАЧАЛЬНИКИ ЛАГЕРЕЙ ГУЛАГА НА КОЛЫМЕ, 501-505 И ДРУГИХ СТРОЙКАХ С ЦЕЛЬЮ „СОКРАЩЕНИЯ ЧИСЛА ЗЭКОВ"И ПОДНЯТИЯ ТРУДОВОЙ ДИСЦИПЛИНЫ ВВЕЛИ ЗВЕРСКОЕ ПРАВИЛО –„ БЕЗ ПОСЛЕДНЕГО," Т.Е. РАССТРЕЛИВАЛСЯ КАЖДЫЙ ЗЭК, КОТОРЫЙ СТАНОВИЛСЯ ПОСЛЕДНИМ В СТРОЙ РАБОЧИХ БРИГАД ПО КОМАНДЕ „НА РАБОТУ СТАНОВИСЬ!" И ТАКИМ ОБРАЗОМ КАЖДЫЙ ДЕНЬ УНИЧТОЖАЛИСЬ „ПОСЛЕДНИЕ"...)

The bestial rule of 'minus the last one'. Fifteen seconds before 'reduction'.

'Please chief! Spare me! I have three kids, a wife and a sick mother at home.'
'I can't. I have orders not to spare the lives of enemies of the people.'
Some wardens of the Gulag camps in Kolyma, construction sites Nos. 501–505, and some others, in order to 'reduce the number of prisoners' and to improve work discipline, introduced a bestial rule they called 'minus the last one'. The prisoners who were last to line up after the 'Line up for work!' command were shot. Every day the 'last' prisoner was killed.

В СЛОН С ГОРЫ СЕКИРНОЙ СПУСКАЛИ ЗЭКОВ, ПРИВЯЗАННЫХ К БРЕВНУ, ПО ЛЕСТНИЦЕ В 365 СТУПЕНЕК. ЛЕСТНИЦУ НАЗЫВАЛИ: „ГОДОВОЙ,” „МОЛОТИЛКОЙ,” „ЛЕСТНИЦЕЙ СМЕРТИ,” „ДОРОГОЙ В РАЙ.” ЖЕРТВАМИ СТАНОВИЛИСЬ ОБЫЧНО ЗАКЛЮЧЁННЫЕ ИЗ „КЛАССОВЫХ ВРАГОВ.” В КОНЦЕ СПУСКА ИХ ТЕЛА ПРЕВРАЩАЛИСЬ В КРОВАВОЕ МЕСИВО...

In the Solovki Special Prison Camp (SLON), prisoners were tied to a heavy log and thrown down the 365 stairs of the Sekirnaya Mound. The stairs had different nicknames, such as: 'The Year-Long Stairs', 'The Thresher', 'The Stairs of Death' and 'The Road to Heaven'. The victims of the stairs were usually 'class enemy' convicts. By the time the victims reached the bottom, their bodies had turned into a bloody, unrecognisable pulp.

НАКАЗАНИЕ ЗЭКА ЗА НЕПОВИНОВЕНИЕ И НАПАДЕНИЕ НА РАБОТНИКА АДМИНИСТРАЦИИ ЛАГЕРЯ...

В УЧРЕЖДЕНИЯХ ГУЛАГА ЗАКЛЮЧЕННЫЕ ПОДВЕРГАЛИСЬ ЖЕСТОЧАЙШИМ НАКАЗАНИЯМ ЗА НАПАДЕНИЕ НА РАБОТНИКОВ ИТЛ, СОПРОТИВЛЕНИЕ РЕЖИМУ СОДЕРЖАНИЯ, ОТКАЗ ОТ РАБОТЫ, ВПЛОТЬ ДО РАССТРЕЛА ИЛИ УМЕРЩВЛЕНИЯ ГОЛОДОМ В ШИЗО (ШТРАФНОМ ИЗОЛЯТОРЕ)...

Punishment of a convict for disobedience or an assault on the prison authorities.

In the Gulag penal institutions, prisoners were punished severely for assaults on prison authorities or other employees, disobedience, or refusal to work. Punishments varied, but ranged all the way up to execution or forced starvation to death in the SHIZO (isolation cells).

РАССТРЕЛ РАБОТНИКАМИ ИТЛ ГУЛАГА "ВРАГОВ НАРОДА, ИЗОБЛИЧЕННЫХ В ФАШИСТСКОМ ЗАГОВОРЕ..."

В 1941-45 г.г. РУКОВОДИТЕЛИ ИТЛ ГУЛАГА, БОЯСЬ ПОПАСТЬ НА ФРОНТ, СЛАЛИ В НКВД СССР ФАЛЬСИФИЦИРОВАННЫЕ ДОНЕСЕНИЯ О "РАСКРЫТИИ И ЛИКВИДАЦИИ ЗАГО-ВОРОВ ВРАГОВ НАРОДА," КОТОРЫЕ ПЫТАЛИСЬ: 1. РАЗОРУЖИТЬ И УБИТЬ ОХРАНУ И АДМИНИСТРАЦИЮ ИТЛ. 2. ЗАХВАТИТЬ ТРАНСПОРТ И ПРОРВАТЬСЯ НА СОЕДИНЕ-НИЕ С ФАШИСТАМИ. 3. ВЗРЫВАТЬ ЗАВОДЫ И ФАБРИКИ, СНАБЖАЮЩИЕ ФРОНТ. 4. ЖЕЧЬ ПРОДОВОЛЬСТВЕННЫЕ СКЛАДЫ. 5. УНИЧТОЖАТЬ Ж.Д. ПУТИ, МОСТЫ, ПО КОТО-РЫМ СНАБЖАЮТСЯ ВОЙСКА ФРОНТОВ. 6. ВЕСТИ БОИ В ТЫЛУ СССР. 7. УЙТИ ЗА РУБЕЖ...

Execution by firing squad of the 'enemies of the people' exposed as 'fascist plotters' by Gulag guards.

Between 1941 and 1945 [when the USSR was fighting the Second World War], the authorities of the Gulag prison camp, afraid of being sent to the front line, sent falsified reports to the NKVD. They claimed to have 'exposed and stopped conspiracies undertaken by enemies of the people' who had attempted the following actions: 1. To disarm and kill the guards and the prison administration. 2. To capture transportation and break through to join the fascist forces. 3. To blow up plants and factories that produced supplies for the Soviet Army. 4. To burn down food supply warehouses. 5. To destroy railroads and bridges, used to deliver supplies to the soldiers at the front line. 6. To engage in warfare on the home front of the USSR. 7. To escape abroad, etc.

УГОЛОВНИК-БРИГАДИР „ВОСПИТЫВАЕТ" ИНТЕЛЛИГЕНТОВ...

– Я ВАС, ПРОФЕССОРОВ, АКАДЕМИКОВ И ВСЯКИХ ИНТЕЛЛИ-
ГЕНТИКОВ „ПРИДУРКОВ" НАУЧУ ВКАЛЫВАТЬ В ЗОНЕ! БУДЕ-
ТЕ ДЕЛАТЬ ПО ТРИ НОРМЫ!... ВСЕХ ГАДОВ ЗАМОЧУ!...

A foreman convict 'teaches' the intellectuals.

'I'll teach you professors, academics and other eggheads how to sweat your guts out in prison! You're gonna be doing three quotas a day! I'll kill all you bastards!'

* Most intellectuals were 'political' prisoners sentenced under Article 58 (see page 81). Officially they were forbidden to occupy 'trustee' positions where their abilities might be put to some use; instead they were made to do physical work. They had to rapidly adapt to survive or the camp system would quickly crush them.

РАСПРОСТРАНЕННЫЙ ВИД НАКАЗАНИЯ В *ГУЛАГЕ* ЗА НАРУШЕНИЕ РЕЖИМА – „*НА МОШКУ (КОМАРА, ГНУСА)*"...

НАЧАЛЬСТВО И ОХРАНА ЛАГЕРЕЙ ЗА НЕВЫПОЛНЕНИЕ НОРМЫ ВЫРАБОТКИ И ОСЛУШАНИЕ ЗЭКОВ „ВРАГОВ НАРОДА" ПРИ АКТИВНОМ УЧАСТИИ ВЕРНЫХ СВОИХ ПОМОЩНИКОВ УГОЛОВНИКОВ-УРОК РАЗДЕВАЛИ ЖЕРТВЫ ДОГОЛА И ПРИВЯЗЫВАЛИ К ДЕРЕВЬЯМ.   ЗА НЕСКОЛЬКО ЧАСОВ ЛЮДИ ТЕРЯЛИ МНОГО КРОВИ, ТЕЛА ИХ РАСПУХАЛИ И ЧАСТО НАСТУПАЛА СМЕРТЬ...

A widespread punishment in the Gulag for breaching internal prison regulations was called 'Gnat Bait' (also 'Mosquito Bait', 'Midge Bait').

For failure to meet labour quotas and for disobedience, the prison authorities and guards, with the help from their loyal assistants – the *urkas*, stripped the 'enemies of the people' naked and tied them to trees. In a matter of hours the victims lost a great deal of blood. Their bodies swelled up, and the outcome was often death.

НЕКОТОРЫЕ ИЗУВЕРЫ ГУЛАГА В ГОДЫ КУЛЬТА,РАДИ ПОТЕХИ,ЖЕНЩИН ИЗ КОНТИНГЕНТА„ВРАГОВ НАРОДА" ЗА„ПРОВИННОСТЬ" САЖАЛИ НА МУРАВЕЙНИКИ...

МОЛОДЫХ ЖЕНЩИН ОТКАЗАВШИХСЯ БЫТЬ ЛЮБОВНИЦАМИ ПАЛАЧЕЙ ГУЛАГА, САЖАЛИ НА МУРАВЕЙНИКИ,ПРИВЯЗЫВАЛИ К ДЕРЕВЬЯМ,НА КОМАРЫ И МУРАВЬЯМ."ИНОГДА ВО ВЛАГАЛИЩЕ ВСТАВЛЯЛИ РАСТИТЕЛЬНУЮ ТРУБКУ-ДУДКУ ИЛИ БЕРЕСТУ, СВЁРНУТУЮ ТРУБКОЙ ДЛЯ ВХОДА МУРАВЬЯМ, НА НО-ГИ ПРИВЯЗЫВАЛИ РАСПЯЛКУ.ЧАСТО ПАЛАЧАМ ПОМОГАЛИ ЗЭЧКИ-ВОРОВКИ...

During the cult of personality, some sadistic guards, for their own entertainment, put women 'enemies of the people' on ant hills for 'infractions'.

Young women who refused to be the concubines of the Gulag executioners were put on ant hills and tied to a tree. Sometimes, a tube made out of birch bark or another kind of hollow tube, was inserted into the vagina so the ants could crawl inside. The legs were fixed with a pole. Female criminals often assisted the guards.

Escapees and Deniers

С ПРИВОЗОМ В ИТЛ ГУЛАГА БЫВШИХ ФРОНТОВИКОВ 2Й
ИЗ ЗАПАДНОЙ ЕВРОПЫ, УЧАСТИЛИСЬ ЛАГЕРНЫЕ БУНТЫ И
ЦИИ. БУНТЫ ЗЭКОВ ПОДАВЛЯЛИСЬ ЖЕСТОЧАЙШИМИ МЕР

ЕННИМИ ВОЙСКАМИ МВД И ТАНКАМИ. 1947 г. ...

ТНЫ, ПЛЕНЁННЫХ И ДЕПОРТИРОВАННЫХ ГРАЖДАН СССР
КОГО ОТНОШЕНИЯ К ЗЭКАМ СО СТОРОНЫ АДМИНИСТРА-

The suppression of a revolt in the camp using internal troops of the MVD and tanks.* 1947.

After the Second World War, many soldiers, POWs and citizens of the USSR were deported from Europe and sent to the Gulag camps. The number of prison revolts due to the inhumane practises of the administration toward prisoners increased. The revolts were suppressed with brute force.

* 'The sociology of the political prisoners had also undergone changes: the place of a large percentage of the meek victims of the Great Terror was taken by yesterday's tough soldiers and by people from the recently annexed territories. The loyal supporters of the regime still remaining behind barbed wire were now outnumbered by active non-conformers... Strikes broke out in many camps, often leading to rebellions; they were brutally suppressed, sometimes with the use of tanks, though "diplomacy" was resorted to in moderate cases (Filshtinsky 1994).' Leona Toker, *Return from the Archipelago*, 2000.

НАКАЗАНИЕ БЕГЛЕЦОВ ПОСЛЕ РОЗЫСКА, ЗАДЕРЖАНИЯ. ПРИ ОКАЗАНИИ МАЛЕЙШЕГО СОПРОТИВЛЕНИЯ ЕДВА НЕ РАЗОДРАННЫЕ РОЗЫСКНОЙ СОБАКОЙ БЕГЛЕЦЫ ДОБИВАЛИСЬ ОХРАНОЙ. ЧТОБЫ НЕ ВОЗИТЬСЯ С ТРУПАМИ И НЕ ДОСТАВЛЯТЬ УБИТЫХ В ЛАГЕРЬ, КИСТИ РУК У НИХ ОТРЕЗАЛИСЬ ДЛЯ ДАКТИЛОСКОПИРОВАНИЯ И СПИСАНИЯ УБИТЫХ В ИТЛ ГУЛАГА... ("ШУТНИКИ" ИНОГДА ОТРЕЗАЛИ УШИ)

Punishment of escapees after they were found and caught. If they showed the least bit of resistance, escapees, nearly torn to shreds by dogs, were finished off by the guards. So they didn't have to bring the bodies back to the prison camp, the guards cut off the dead escapees' hands for fingerprinting and for writing them off at the Gulag[*]. (Some 'jokers' often cut off the escapees' ears.)

[*] Varlam Shalamov describes how a Corporal Postnikov ambushed and killed an escaped convict, six miles from the mine at Arklagla: 'Postnikov took an axe and chopped off both hands at the wrist so that bookkeeping could take fingerprints. He put the hands in his pouch and set off home to write up the latest report on a successful hunt… That night the dead man got up and with the bloody stumps of his forearms pressed to his chest somehow reached the tent in which the convict-labourers lived. His pale face drained of blood, he stood at the doorway and peered in with unusually blue, crazed eyes. Bent double and leaning against the doorframe, he glared from under lowered brows and groaned. He was shaking terribly. Black blood spotted his quilted jacket, his pants, and his rubber boots. He was given some hot soup, and his terrible wrists were wrapped in rags. Fellow prisoners started to take him to the first-aid station but Corporal Postnikov himself, along with some soldiers, came running from the hut that served as the outpost. The soldiers took the man off somewhere – but not to the hospital or the first-aid station. I never heard anything more of the prisoner with the chopped-off hands.' Varlam Shalamov, *Kolyma Tales*, 1980.

–ТЫ, ЧЕРНОЖОПИК, И ТЫ, МОРДА ЖИДОВСКАЯ, СРУБИТЕ ВОН ТЕ КУСТЫ!...
–НАЧАЛЬНИК, ВЕДЬ ЗАСТРЕЛИШЬ? ЭТО ЖЕ ЗА ФЛАЖКАМИ ЗОНЫ...
КАК ТОЛЬКО ЗЭКИ ВЫХОДИЛИ ЗА ОХРАНЯЕМУЮ ЗОНУ, РАЗДАВАЛАСЬ КОМАНДА „БРИГАДА, ЛОЖИСЬ!,"
И СПИНЫ „БЕГЛЕЦОВ" ПО УСТАВУ МВД ПРОШИВАЛА АВТОМАТНАЯ ОЧЕРЕДЬ... ПРЕМИЯ – 40 РУБЛЕЙ

'Hey you, black-arse, and you, yid! Go and chop down those bushes over there!'
'But, chief, you're going to shoot us! It's outside the flagged zone.'
As soon as the prisoners strolled beyond guarded territory, the guards commanded, 'Brigade, get down!' and a burst of machine-gun fire hit the backs of the 'escapees', in accordance with the regulations of the MVD.[*]
The bonus was forty rubles.

[*] 'I was working with Rybakov, who was gathering berries in a tin can during the rest periods, and whenever Seroshapka [the guard] looked the other way. If Rybakov could manage to fill the can, the guards' cook would give him some bread. Rybakov's undertaking began to assume major dimensions... While working and gathering berries, we had approached the border of the forbidden 'zone', without even noticing it. The markers were hanging right over our heads... Ahead, however, were hummocks of sweet-brier, cowberry, and blueberry... Rybakov pointed at his can, not yet full, and at the sun, slowly setting on the horizon. Slowly he crept toward the enchanted berries. I heard the dry crack of a shot, and Rybakov fell face down among the hummocks. Seroshapka waved his rifle and shouted: "Leave him there, don't go near him." Seroshapka cocked his rifle and shot in the air. We knew what this second shot meant. Seroshapka also knew. There were supposed to be two shots – the first one a warning.' Varlam Shalamov, *Kolyma Tales*, 1980.

ДОСТАВКА УБИТОГО „ВРАГА НАРОДА" ПРИ ПОБЕГЕ В ИТЛ ГУЛАГА ГРУППОЙ ЗАКЛЮЧЁННЫХ ПОД КОНВОЕМ...

ИНОГДА УБИТОГО ПОБЛИЗОСТИ ОТ ИТЛ БЕГЛЕЦА ДЕМОНСТРАТИВНО НЕС-
ЛИ В ЗОНУ НА ШЕСТЕ (ЖЕРДИ) КАК КАБАНА ИЛИ КОСУЛЮ НА БОЯРСКОЙ
ОХОТЕ, ЧТО ПРОИЗВОДИЛО НА ЗАКЛЮЧЁННЫХ УДРУЧАЮЩИЙ ЭФФЕКТ.
   У УБИТОГО БЕГЛЕЦА ВДАЛИ ОТ ИТЛ ОТРЕЗАЛИ КИСТИ РУК ДЛЯ ДАКТИ-
ЛОСКОПИРОВАНИЯ И СПИСАНИЯ ЗЭКА. ТРУП ОСТАВЛЯЛИ В ТАЙГЕ, ТУНДРЕ...

An 'enemy of the people', killed after trying to escape, is delivered back to the Gulag prison camp by a group of convicts and guards.

Occasionally, when an escapee was killed close to the prison, his body was demonstratively brought back into the camp on a stick, like a wild boar or a deer after a hunt. The spectacle was very dispiriting for the prisoners. If an escapee was killed far away from the camp, his hands were cut off for fingerprinting and writing off. The body was left out in the taiga or tundra.

УБИЙСТВО УГОЛОВНИКОМ „БЫЧКА" ПРИ ПОБЕГЕ ИЗ ИТЛ...

УГОЛОВНИКИ ПРИ ПОБЕГАХ ИЗ ДАЛЬНИХ СЕВЕРНЫХ ЛАГЕРЕЙ ГУЛАГА СМАНИВАЛИ С СОБОЙ (ИЗ-ЗА НЕВОЗМОЖНОСТИ ЗАПАСТИСЬ ПРОДУКТАМИ В УСЛОВИЯХ ИТЛ) ДРУГИХ ЗЭКОВ, КОТОРЫХ УБИВАЛИ В ПУТИ. ТАКИЕ ЖЕРТВЫ ЛЮДОЕДСТВА НА УГОЛОВНОМ ЖАРГОНЕ НАЗЫВАЛИСЬ „БЫЧКАМИ." СКОЛЬКО СЪЕДЕНО ТАКИХ „БЫЧКОВ," НЕИЗВЕСТНО...

A criminal kills a 'calf' during a prison escape.

Because they could not store food while in prison, criminals in remote northern prison camps of the Gulag[*] would coax another inmate to run away with them.[†] They then killed them in the taiga. The slang word for these victims of cannibalism was *bychok* ('calf'). It is impossible to say for certain how many 'calves' were eaten.

[*] The remoteness of the Kolyma region took on mystical status among its inmates, who referred to it as the 'planet'. 'Kolyma, Kolyma / Wonderful planet! / Twelve months of winter, / The rest summer.': Kolyma prisoners' song.
[†] 'When you have a huge community of people who dream of nothing but escape, it is inevitable that every possible means of doing so will be discussed. A "walking supply" is, in fact, a fat prisoner. If you have to, you can kill him and eat him. And until you need him, he is carrying the "food" himself.' Edward Buca, *Vorkuta*, 1976.

An incident in the art shop of the Dalstroy* Gulag prison camp. 1949.
Vertical signs on the left read (incomplete): **'The MVD is the Guardian of Public Order in [...]'**; **'The Gulag is the Foundation of [...]'**; **Socialist [...]'**. Vertical signs on the right read (incomplete): **'Enemies of the USSR!'**; **'VKP(b)!'**. Verse on the poster on the right reads: **'Shut up, Europe / You total fool! / Comrade Murlo[†] / Is laughing at you. / Fat-bestial,[‡] / Narrow-minded. / Europeans, / On what did you spread your powdery pollen? V. Mayakovsky'**. Horizontal signs read (top to bottom): **'Long Live Communism – the Bright Future of All Humanity'**; **'One of the Testaments of the Great Leader of the Proletariat was: Suffer, Suffer, and Suffer Again. V. I. Lenin'**. [Note: The original quote by Lenin was 'Study, study, and study again.' The word *uchitsya* (to study) has been altered by adding the letter *m* and a stress mark, so it reads *muchitsya* (to suffer). **'May the Great Revolutionary Teachings of Marx, Engels, Lenin, and Stalin Live Forever!'**.[§]

'Are you out of your mind? Do you want a bullet in the forehead for this rubbish?'
'Comrade Major, it's not our fault! Someone crept into the shop and added those *M*'s.'

* Dalstroy (the Far North Construction Trust) was created by the NKVD to oversee the development of an infrastructure to support gold mining activities in the Kolyma region. During its lifespan (1932-1953) Dalstroy established around eighty Gulag camps for this purpose.

† The lines are from the poem *The Movie Fad* (*Kinopovetrie*) by Vladimir Mayakovsky. Some words have been altered, however. The 'Comrade Charlot' of the original (Charlie Chaplin's eponymous character in *The Tramp* (1915), was known as *Charlot* in many European countries) has been altered to read 'Comrade Murlo', i.e. 'Comrade Ugly Face'.

‡ Another alteration of the text. The original poem uses the word *zhirnozhivotye* (fat-belly); here the letter *n* has been added so it reads *zhirnozhivotnye* (fat-bestial).

§ Propaganda was a part of everyday Soviet life, ubiquitous in film, radio, posters, placards and wall-papers (paper was in short supply so sheet versions of newspapers were pasted onto walls). The authorities found more unusual places to locate their slogans. Carved into rock in Magadan: 'Glory to Stalin, the Greatest Genius of Mankind', 'Glory to Stalin the Best Friend of the Workers and Peasants', etc. Also recently discovered through Google Earth, a 600 metre long message 'celebrating' Lenin's anniversary: 'Lenin 100 Years'. Made in 1970 by felling timber in a Siberian forest, the trees left standing form the letters. Only visible from the sky, it has been suggested it was 'constructed' specifically for American spy satellites.

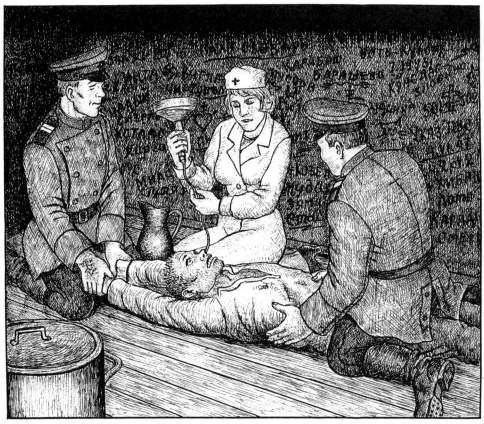

НАСИЛЬСТВЕННОЕ КОРМЛЕНИЕ ЗАКЛЮЧЁННОГО, ОБЪЯВИВШЕГО ГОЛОДОВ- КУ ПИТАТЕЛЬНОЙ СМЕСЬЮ ЧЕРЕЗ НОЗДРЮ... ПО ЗАКОНАМ СОВЕТСКОГО ГУМАНИЗМА ПУСКАТЬ ПУЛЮ В ЗАТЫЛОК МОЖНО ТОЛЬКО ЗДОРОВОЙ ЖЕРТВЕ С ТЕМПЕРАТУРОЙ ТЕЛА 36,6 -37:..

Force-feeding a prisoner on a hunger strike[*] with a nutrient solution through the nostril.
According to the most 'humane' Soviet laws, only a healthy individual with a body temperature of 36.6° to 37° C could be shot in the head.

[*] 'For the first few days, no one takes a blind bit of notice. Then, after several days – sometimes as many as ten or twelve – they transfer you to a special cell set aside for such people, and start to feed you artificially, through a pipe. It is useless to resist, for whatever you do they twist your arms behind your back and handcuff you. This procedure is usually carried out in the camps even more brutally than in remand prison – by the time you've been force-fed once or twice you are often minus your teeth…' Anatoly Marchenko, *My Testimony*, 1969. Marchenko died in prison in 1986 following complications after an extended hunger strike.

– ЗАТЯНИ-КА МОЮ КУЛЬТЮ, И Я РВАНУ В САНЧАСТЬ НА ПЕРЕВЯЗКУ!...
УГОЛОВНИКИ, ЧАЩЕ ВОРЫ, ЧТОБЫ ИЗБАВИТЬСЯ ОТ ТЯЖЕЛЫХ
ОБЩИХ РАБОТ, ОТРУБАЛИ СЕБЕ ПАЛЬЦЫ, КИСТЬ РУКИ, ГЛОТАЛИ ЛОЖКИ,
ГВОЗДИ И Т.Д., В ИТЛ ГУЛАГА ИХ НАЗЫВАЛИ – „САМОРУБ", „МАСТЫРЩИК" И Т.Д.

'Bind up my stump real tight now, and I'm going to run to the hospital to have it dressed.'

To avoid hard labour, criminals, usually thieves, often cut off their own fingers or hands,* swallowed spoons or nails, etc.† They were called *samorubs* (self cutters) or *mastyrshchiks* (maimers) in the Gulag prison camps.

* 'One prisoner tells the story of a thief who cut off four fingers of his left hand. Instead of being sent to an invalid camp, however, the invalid was made to sit in the snow and watch as others worked. Forbidden to move around, on pain of being shot for attempted escape, "very soon he himself requested a shovel and, moving it like a crutch, with his surviving hand, poked at the frozen earth, crying and swearing."' Anne Applebaum, *Gulag: A History*, 2003.

† 'I have many times witnessed some of the most fantastic incidences of self-mutilation. I have seen convicts swallow huge numbers of nails and barbed wire; I have seen them swallow mercury thermometers, pewter tureens (after first breaking them up into "edible" proportions), chess pieces, dominoes, needles, ground glass, spoons, knives and many other similar objects; I have seen convicts sew up their mouths or eyes with thread or wire; sew rows of buttons to their bodies; or nail testicles to a bed, swallow a nail bent like a hook, and then attach this hook to a door by way of a thread so the door cannot be opened without pulling the "fish" inside out. I have seen convicts cut open the skin on their arms and legs and peel it off as if it were a stocking … or cover themselves with paper and set fire to themselves; or cut off their fingers, or their nose, or ears, or penis…' Edward Kuznetsov, *Prison Diaries*, 1975.

The Country Becomes a Gulag

ГОЛОД-ЛЮБИМОЕ ДЕТИЩЕ И ВЕЧНЫЙ СПУТНИК КПСС

В 1930-33 ГГ. КОММУНИСТЫ В БОРЬБЕ С „КЛАССОВЫМ ВРАГОМ" СОЗДАЛИ ИСКУССТВЕННЫЙ ГОЛОД НА УКРАИНЕ, В БЕЛОРУССИИ, КАЗАХСТАНЕ, СИБИРИ И ДР. РЕГИОНАХ ПУТЕМ ПОЛНОГО ВЫВОЗА ХЛЕБА, КРУПЫ, МАСЛА, СКОТА И Т.Д. С ПРИМЕНЕНИЕМ ВОЙСК ГПУ-ДЛЯ ПРОДАЖИ ЗА ГРАНИЦУ. НАРОДУ СТРАНЫ ЭТА КОНФИСКАЦИЯ СТОИЛА 12-13 МИЛЛИОНОВ ЖИЗНЕЙ...

Famine – dearest child and companion of the Communist Party.

Between 1930 and 1933, the Communists artificially created a great famine in Ukraine, Byelorussia, Kazakhstan, Siberia, and other regions, in order to fight the 'class enemy'. They used GPU troops to take bread, grain, butter and cattle by force, and then sold the goods abroad.[*] This expropriation cost the lives of twelve to thirteen million ordinary people.[†§]

[*] The grain confiscation and its subsequent export was vital for the Soviet Union. The hard currency generated by its sale was used to buy machinery essential for the compulsive collectivization of the country.
[†] Although it is impossible to gauge the death toll of this famine accurately, modern sources set the figure between six to eight million.
[§] 'In the morning horses pulled flat-top carts through the city and the corpses of those who had died in the night were collected. I saw one such flat-top cart with children lying on it. They were just as I have described them, thin, elongated faces, like those of dead birds, with sharp beaks. These tiny birds had flown into Kiev and what good had it done them? Some of them were still muttering, and their heads still turning. I asked the driver about them, and he just waved his hands and said: 'By the time they get where they are being taken they will be silent too.' Vasily Grossman, *Forever Flowing*, 1972, (quoted by: Robert Conquest, *The Harvest of Sorrow: Soviet Collectivization and the Terror-Famine*, 1986).

„САНИТАРНЫЙ ОТСТРЕЛ" РАБОТНИКАМИ НКВД ПАРТИЙНЫХ И ДР. КАДРОВ НАЦИОНАЛЬНЫХ РЕСПУБЛИК СССР...

В ГОДЫ СТАЛИНИЗМА ПЕРИОДИЧЕСКИ ПРОИЗВОДИЛИСЬ, С ЦЕЛЬЮ ПРОФИЛАКТИКИ ВОЗНИКНОВЕНИЯ НАЦИОНАЛЬНОГО ПРАВОСОЗНАНИЯ У НЕРУССКИХ НАРОДОВ, ВЫБОРОЧНЫЕ РАССТРЕЛЫ ПАРТИЙНЫХ, СОВЕТСКИХ, ХОЗЯЙСТВЕННЫХ И ТВОРЧЕСКИХ РАБОТНИКОВ ПО КОМАНДЕ ИЗ ЦЕНТРА, И ДАЖЕ СПУСКАЛИСЬ РАЗНАРЯДКИ НА КОЛИЧЕСТВО „ГОЛОВ," ПОДОБНО ОХОТНИЧЬИМ ЛИЦЕНЗИЯМ НА ОТСТРЕЛ ЗВЕРЕЙ ПО ВИДАМ – ЛОСЕЙ, САЙГАКОВ, КАБАНОВ, АРХАРОВ, МЕДВЕДЕЙ И Т. Д.

The 'sanitary shootings' of Party members and other executives of the USSR republics by the NKVD.

During the Stalin era targeted executions were carried out by order of the Centre, in order to discourage aspirations of national identity and rights among non-Russians. Victims included Party members, Soviet employees, economic organisations, and artists. Sometimes an order would include a required number of 'head,' similar to a hunting license for killing different animals: elk, saigas, boars, wild rams, bears, etc.

−ВАШИ ДЕДЫ, БАБУШКИ, БРАТЬЯ, СЕСТРЫ, ЖЁНЫ, ДЕТИ И ДРУГИЕ РОДСТВЕ
РОДИНЫ И СТАРШЕГО БРАТА−ВЕЛИКОГО РУССКОГО НАРОДА! ПРИКАЗЫВАЮ СДАТ

ОМ ТЫЛУ НАШЕЙ КРАСНОЙ АРМИИ ВСТАЛИ НА ПУТЬ ПРЕДАТЕЛЕЙ СОВЕТСКОЙ
ИЕ, ОРДЕНА И МЕДАЛИ! ПРИ СОПРОТИВЛЕНИИ БУДЕТЕ РАССТРЕЛЯНЫ НА МЕСТЕ!

1944. The arrest and deportation to the Gulag of the 'traitor' soldiers of the Second World War: Kalmyks, Ingushes, Chechens and others.
The sign reads: **'Warsaw 500 km'**.

'Your grandfathers, grandmothers, sisters, wives, children and other relatives on the home front of the Red Army started down the path of traitors of the Soviet Motherland and its older brother – the great Soviet people! I hereby command you to lay down your guns, decorations and medals! If you resist arrest you will be shot dead on the spot.'

ВОЕНИЗИРОВАННОЕ ПОДРАЗДЕЛЕНИЕ ИЗ ЗЭКОВ ГУЛАГа...

ПЕРЕД ВОЙНОЙ В 1939-40 гг. ПО УКАЗАНИЮ И.СТАЛИНА, Л.БЕРИЯ СФОРМИРОВАЛ ИЗ
ЗЭКОВ 6-7 КРУПНЫХ ВОЕНИЗИРОВАННЫХ СОЕДИНЕНИЙ, КОТОРЫЕ ПОСЛЕ КРАТ-
КОЙ ПОДГОТОВКИ В СПЕЦИАЛЬНЫХ ЛАГЕРЯХ СИБИРИ И УРАЛА (ВООРУЖЕННЫЕ
ТОЛЬКО СТРЕЛКОВЫМ ОРУЖИЕМ) СКРЫТНО БЫЛИ ПОДТЯНУТЫ К ЗАПАДНЫМ ГРА-
НИЦАМ. ЭТО БЫЛИ СОЕДИНЕНИЯ ПЕРВОГО УДАРА („ПУШЕЧНОЕ МЯСО") С ПОДРАЗДЕ-
ЛЕНИЯМИ ТАНКОДЕСАНТНИКОВ НА БТ-7, БТ-8 С 45 ММ ПУШКАМИ И АВИАЦИОННЫМИ
МОТОРАМИ (ТАНКИ ТИПА „КРИСТИ"), РАЗВИВАЮЩИМИ СКОРОСТЬ НА ХОРОШИХ ДОРО-
ГАХ ДО 110 КМ В ЧАС. В 1941г. В ПЕРВЫЙ МЕСЯЦ ВОЙНЫ ЭТИ ВОЕНИЗИРОВАННЫЕ
СОЕДИНЕНИЯ ИЗ ЗЭКОВ ГУЛАГА БЫЛИ РАЗГРОМЛЕНЫ И ПЛЕНЕНЫ НЕМЕЦКО-
ФАШИСТСКИМИ ВОЙСКАМИ, Т.К. НЕ МОГЛИ ОКАЗАТЬ СЕРЬЁЗНОГО СОПРОТИВЛЕ-
НИЯ ИЗ-ЗА ПЛОХОГО ВООРУЖЕНИЯ И СЛАБОЙ БОЕВОЙ ПОДГОТОВКИ...

An armed unit made up of Gulag convicts.

By the order of Joseph Stalin, in 1939 and 1940, right before the start of the Second World War, Lavrenty Beria formed six or seven large armed units made up of prisoners. After brief training at specialised boot camps in Siberia and the Urals, armed only with rifles and handguns, they were secretly transported to the western borders of the USSR. These were the 'first hit' units – cannon fodder – sent before the regiments on diesel engined BT-7 and BT-8 tanks with 45 mm cannons (based on the Christie tank). The tanks were very mobile and could reach speeds of 110 km/h on a good road surface. In 1941, during the first month of the war, these armed units of Gulag convicts were defeated and taken as prisoners of war by the German forces. They were unable to put up any real resistance due to poor training and insufficient armaments.

ИЗ ГИТЛЕРОВСКОГО АДА В СТАЛИНСКИЙ СОЦИАЛИСТИЧЕСКИЙ РАЙ...
-ВАС ПРИВЕЗЛИ В НАШ ГУЛАГ КАК ПРЕДАТЕЛЕЙ РОДИНЫ! ВЫ ВСЕ ПОС-
ЛЕ РАНЕНИЯ ПОПАЛИ В ПЛЕН В 1941 ГОДУ! ВМЕСТО БОРЬБЫ ДО ПОС-
ЛЕДНЕГО ВЗДОХА И КАПЛИ КРОВИ ОТСИЖИВАЛИСЬ НА СЫТЫХ НЕ-
МЕЦКО-ФАШИСТСКИХ ПАЙКАХ В БУХЕНВАЛЬДЕ, ОСВЕНЦИМЕ, ДАХАУ!
ВЫ ВСЕ СВОЕЙ ТРУСОСТЬЮ ОПОЗОРИЛИ НАШУ КРАСНУЮ АРМИЮ...

From Hitler's hell to Stalin's socialist heaven.

'You were brought to the Gulag because you are traitors to the Motherland. You were all taken prisoner of war after you were wounded in 1941.[*] Instead of fighting to the last drop of blood, to the last breath, you were fattening yourself up on nutritious German Fascist rations in Buchenwald, Auschwitz and Dachau! With your cowardice, you have shamed our Red Amy!'[†]

[*] Prisoners of war who returned to Russia after the Second World War were viewed as traitors. They were transported directly to the Gulag and handed long sentences for their supposed cowardice.
[†] Baldaev has ironically given the camp commander the characteristics of Leon Trotsky – founder and commander of the Red Army. One of the original leaders of the October Revolution of 1917, he was murdered in exile in 1940. Under orders from Stalin, a KGB agent fatally wounded him with an ice axe.

—НУ И ЖИВУЧИ ЭТИ НАЦИОНАЛИСТЫ, ТРИ НЕДЕЛИ ВЕЗЕМ, А У ЭТИХ ЧУХО-
НОК ЕЩЕ ИХ ЩЕНКИ ЖИВЫЕ! КАК КОНЧИТСЯ ИХ ЖРАТВА, ВСЕ ДУБА ДАДУТ...
„НАЦИОНАЛИСТАМИ" БЫЛИ: ЭСТОНЦЫ, ЛИТОВЦЫ, ЛАТЫШИ, УКРАИНЦЫ,
ЧЕЧЕНЫ, КАЛМЫКИ, НЕМЦЫ... И РАЗНЫЕ ПРОЧИЕ НЕРУССКИЕ ...

'Damn nationals just wouldn't die. We've been transporting them for three weeks now, and even their little bastards are still alive! But that's okay. Once they run out of food, they're all going to kick the bucket.'
The 'nationals' were Estonians, Lithuanians, Latvians, Ukrainians, Chechens, Kalmyks, Germans and various other non-Russians.

В ГОДЫ КУЛЬТА ТЮРЕМНЫЕ КАМЕРЫ С „ВРАГАМИ НАРОДА" БЫЛИ ПОДОБНЫ СЕЛЬДЯНЫМ БОЧКАМ...

АРЕСТОВАННЫЕ БЫЛИ ВЫНУЖДЕНЫ ОТДЫХАТЬ (СПАТЬ) ПО ОЧЕРЕДИ И ПОВОРАЧИВАТЬСЯ ОДНОВРЕМЕННО, ЧТОБЫ НЕ ОТЛЕЖАТЬ БОКА НА КАМЕННОМ ИЛИ БЕТОННОМ ПОЛУ, Т.К. ПОСТЕЛЬ НЕ ВЫДАВАЛАСЬ, И КТО СПАЛ ДНЁМ, ТОТ ЖЕСТОКО НАКАЗЫВАЛСЯ КАРЦЕРОМ И ИЗБИЕНИЕМ...

During the reign of the cult of personality, the 'enemies of the people' were packed into prison cells like sardines in a can.*

Prisoners had to take turns resting (sleeping). They had to turn over all at the same time, so the sides of the body did not go numb lying on the concrete floor. There were no beds in the cells. Those who slept during the day were severely punished with beatings or locked up in an isolation cell.

5 МАРТА 1953Г. ВЕСТЬ О СМЕРТИ СТАЛИНА БЫЛА ВСТ

—УРА! БОЛЬШОЙ ЛЮДОЕД ПОДОХ! РЕБЯТА, МУДРЕЙШИЙ И
ЮЗНОЙ КОММУНИСТИЧЕСКОЙ ПАРТИИ БАНДИТОВ СДО

ИЛЛИОНАМИ ЗЭКОВ ГУЛАГА С БОЛЬШОЙ РАДОСТЬЮ...

ШИХ ОТБРОСИЛ КОПЫТА! УРА! ВОЖДЬ ВКП(б)-ВСЕСО-
ЛИН ДУБА ДАЛ! ДА ЗДРАВСТВУЕТ АМНИСТИЯ! УРА!...

5th March 1953. Millions of Gulag prisoners rejoice at the news of Stalin's death.

'Hooray! The great cannibal has kicked the bucket! Hey fellas, the wisest of the wise is pushing up daisies! Hooray! The leader of the VKP(b) – the All-Union Communist Party of Bandits[*] – pegged out! Hooray! Stalin has danced his last dance! Amnesty[†] is here! Hip-hip hooray!

[*] The prisoners' 'interpretation' of the letter *b*, which officially stood for Bolsheviks.
[†] Initially this amnesty only applied to criminal prisoners and political prisoners with sentences of five years or less (this meant that few political prisoners were actually released, as their terms were usually greater than five years).

Holocaust

МОРСКИЕ БАРЖИ С „ВРАГАМИ НАРОДА"-РАБАМИ ГУЛАГА НКВД-МВД СССР НА ПРОСТОРАХ ОКЕАНА...

ВМЕСТО ВЫПУСКА ИНВАЛИДОВ, БОЛЬНЫХ, ДОХОДЯГ - БЕЗВИННЫХ ЛЮДЕЙ „ВРА-ГОВ НАРОДА" НА СВОБОДУ, ИХ СОТНЯМИ, ТЫСЯЧАМИ ГРУЗИЛИ В СПИСАННЫЕ СТАРЫЕ БАРЖИ И ОТБУКСИРОВЫВАЛИ В МОРЕ, И, КАК ПРАВИЛО, ЭТИ БАРЖИ ТОНУЛИ ОТ „МОРСКОЙ СТИХИИ"-ШТОРМА. ТАК „СОКРАЩАЛОСЬ" ЧИСЛО ЗЭКОВ...

Barges carrying 'enemies of the people', slaves of the Gulag, out to sea.

Instead of discharging the disabled, sick, 'goners' and innocent 'enemies of the people', hundreds and thousands of them were loaded onto old, written-off barges. The barges were then towed out to sea, where they usually sank due to 'the elements' – in storms.[*] This was how the numbers of prisoners were 'reduced'.

[*] Stories of this practise are common although first-hand accounts are scarce: 'Narbut's death was incomparably worse. They say that he was employed in the transit camp to clean out the cesspits and that together with other invalids he was taken out to sea in a barge, which was blown up. This was done to clear the camp of people unable to work. I believe that such things did happen. When I later arrived in Tarusa, there was an old ex-convict called Pavel who used to get water and firewood for me. Without any prompting from me, he once told me how he had witnessed the blowing up of a barge – first they had heard the explosion and then they had seen the barge sinking.' Nadezhda Mandelstam, *Hope Against Hope*, 1999.

ОДИН ИЗ МНОГИХ „ДЕСАНТОВ СМЕРТИ" ИЗ „ВРАГОВ НАРОДА," ВЫСАЖЕННЫЙ ГУЛАГОМ НКВД НА ОДИН ИЗ ПУСТЫННЫХ ОСТРОВОВ АРАЛА ДЛЯ УМЕРЩВЛЕНИЯ БЕЗ ВОДЫ И ПИЩИ... 1938 г.

В 1917 г. КОММУНИСТЫ, ПРИДЯ К ВЛАСТИ, УСТАНОВИЛИ РЕЖИМ ТЕРРОРА. ОНИ ОТНЯЛИ ВСЕ ДЕМОКРАТИЧЕСКИЕ ПРАВА НАРОДОВ РОССИИ. В 1921 г. НА СОЛОВЕЦКИХ ОСТРОВАХ БЫЛИ ЗАМОРЕНЫ ГОЛОДОМ 250 ТЫС. ПЛЕННЫХ БЕЛОЙ АРМИИ, КАЗАКИ ДОНА, КУБАНИ И ТЕРЕКА. В ГОДЫ КУЛЬТА ПРОДОЛЖАЛСЯ ВЫВОЗ СОТЕН ТЫСЯЧ КРЕСТЬЯН – „КУЛАКОВ" И „ВРАГОВ НАРОДА" НА ПУСТЫННЫЕ ОСТРОВА СТРАНЫ ДЛЯ УМЕРЩВЛЕНИЯ ГОЛОДОМ...

One of the many 'troops of death' made up of 'enemies of the people' that the NKVD of the Gulag landed on one of the barren islands of the Aral Sea – and left to die there without food or water. 1938.

In 1917, when the Communists came to power, they established the reign of terror. They took away all democratic rights from the people of Russia. In 1921, 250,000 POWs of the White Army, Cossacks from the Don, Kuban and Terek were left to starve to death on the Solovetsky Islands. The deportation continued during the period of the cult of the personality, when hundreds of thousands of *kulak* peasants and 'enemies of the people' were exiled and also starved to death.

КУРОПАТЫ-БССР.„РАЗДАЧА ЗЕМЛИ КРЕСТЬЯНАМ"

– РОДНЕНЬКИЙ, МОЛЮ, НЕ УБИВАЙ! У МЕНЯ ДОМА
ОСТАЛИСЬ МАЛЕНЬКИЕ ДЕТКИ!
– ЗЕМЛЮ ЗАХОТЕЛА, СЕЙЧАС ЕЁ ПОЛУЧИШЬ ОТ НКВД!...

Kurapaty,* Byelorussian SSR. 'Land for peasants.'

'Son, please don't kill me, for the love of God! I have small children at home!'
'You want land? Here's land for you, courtesy of the NKVD!'

* Kurapaty on the outskirts of Minsk was the site of a mass killing of several thousand civilians between 1937 and 1941. This action was part of a repression of the Byelorusian people, following an attempt by their national leaders to form a breakaway movement from the Soviet Union. The burial sites were not discovered until 1988 and, despite several separate investigations, responsibility for the murders has never been completely established.

УФУ НКВД В ГОДЫ КУЛЬТА ПЕРИОДИЧЕСКИ ПРОИЗВО-ДИЛИСЬ МАССОВЫЕ РАССТРЕЛЫ „ВРАГОВ НАРОДА"...

МАССОВЫЕ „ ПРОФИЛАКТИЧЕСКИЕ ОТСТРЕЛЫ" БОЛЬШЕВИКАМИ НАЧАЛИСЬ В 20-Е ГОДЫ В УСЛОНЕ (УПРАВЛЕНИЕ СОЛОВЕЦКИХ ЛАГЕРЕЙ ОСОБОГО НАЗНАЧЕ-НИЯ)-ОТЦЕ ГУЛАГА. СТАЛИНИЗМ ВСЕГДА ОПАСАЛСЯ ИНТЕЛЛИГЕНТОВ.
В 30-Е ГОДЫ МАССОВЫХ РЕПРЕССИЙ ЭТАПЫ „ВРАГОВ НАРОДА" В ОСНОВНОМ СОСТОЯВШИЕ ИЗ ИНТЕЛЛИГЕНТОВ, ПЕРИОДИЧЕСКИ ОБМАНОМ ВЫВОДИЛИСЬ (ВЫВОЗИЛИСЬ) ОТ НЕСКОЛЬКИХ СОТ ДО ТЫСЯЧ ЧЕЛОВЕК В БЕЗЛЮДНЫЕ СТЕПЬ, ТАЙГУ И ТУНДРУ, ГДЕ ИХ РАССТРЕЛИВАЛИ СПЕЦИАЛЬНЫЕ КОМАНДЫ УФУ НКВД ИЗ СТАНКОВЫХ ПУЛЕМЁТОВ.

During the Stalin era, the UFU NKVD carried out mass-executions of the 'enemies of the people'.

Mass-executions or 'preventative executions' by the Bolsheviks began in the 1920s in the USLON (Department of Specialised Solovki Prison Camps), the 'mother' of the Gulag. Stalinism always feared the intelligentsia. In the 1930s, at the peak of the purges, hundreds and even thousands of 'enemies of the people', mainly intellectuals, were coaxed or forced into the steppes, taiga, or tundra. There they were shot by the UFU NKVD using heavy machine guns.

В КОЛЫМСКИХ ЛАГЕРЯХ БОЛЬНЫХ И СЛАБЫХ МЫЛИ В БАНЕ И ЗА-
ТЕМ ПОД ПРЕДЛОГОМ ВЫДАЧИ БЕЛЬЯ ЧЕРЕЗ ДРУГОЙ ВЫХОД
ЗАГОНЯЛИ ГОЛЫХ И РАСПАРЕННЫХ ПРИ МОРОЗЕ 50° В КЛЕТЬ НА
ТРАКТОРНЫХ САНЯХ И ВЕЗЛИ НА БОЛОТА ДЛЯ ЗАХОРОНЕНИЯ...

In the Kolyma prison camps, the sick and weak were steamed in a sauna. Then – under the pretence of
returning their underwear to them at the opposite exit – they were forced into a cage, naked and steaming after
the sauna, while the temperature outside was 50° C below freezing. The cage with the prisoners was then hauled
away by tractor to a swamp, into which the bodies were thrown.

ПАЛАЧ СЛОН ГУЛАГА НАФТАЛИЙ АРОНОВИЧ ФРЕНКЕЛЬ, КОММУНИСТ, СМОТРЕЛ НА ЛЮДЕЙ, КАК НА „ЧЕЛОВЕЧЕСКИЙ НЕ ОДУШЕВЛЁННЫЙ МАТ-
ЕРИАЛ," ИЗ КОТОРОГО НАДО ВЫЖАТЬ ВСЕ ВОЗМОЖНОЕ И „СПИСАТЬ." В СЛОН ГУЛАГА БОЛЬНЫХ, СТАРЫХ, ИСТОЩЕННЫХ ГОЛОДОМ
И КАТОРЖНОЙ РАБОТОЙ ОХРАНА ПО ПРИКАЗУ НАЧАЛЬСТВА РАЗДЕВАЛА СИЛОЙ И ЗАСТАВЛЯЛА ЛОЖИТЬСЯ НА СНЕГ И ЛЕД ПРИ
МОРОЗЕ В 35-40 ГРАДУСОВ В НАЗИДАНИЕ ДРУГИМ УЗНИКАМ, НЕ ВЫПОЛНЯВШИМ ДНЕВНУЮ НОРМУ. НА МЕСТО УМЕРШИХ ПРИ-
ВОЗИЛИ НОВЫХ. ТАК БЕЗОСТАНОВОЧНО РАБОТАЛ КОНВЕЙЕР СМЕРТИ ГУЛАГА...

The executioner of the Solovki Gulag prison camp, Communist Naftaly Aronovich Frenkel,[*] viewed people as a 'human inanimate matter' that should be squeezed out like a lemon and then written off. In the Solovki Gulag prison camp, the guards, following the orders of the prison authorities, made the elderly prisoners, and those weak from starvation and hard labour, take off their clothes and lie down on snow or ice, while the temperature outside was 35° to 40° C below freezing. This was done for the edification of the other inmates, who didn't fulfil their quotas. This was the lethal conveyor belt of the Gulag in action, operating non-stop.

* Frenkel (1883-1960) first came to the Solovki Gulag as a prisoner. He is often credited with inventing the 'nourishment scale' (the linking of an inmate's ration to their rate of production), which was adopted by the administration. Although this has never been proven, his astonishing rise within the camp system is undisputed. His ideas for turning the camps into profitable institutions came to the attention of Stalin and, following his early release, were used across the Gulag system. Widely hated and feared, he was protected at the highest levels, escaping purges and becoming Chief of Construction for the White Sea Canal where, according to Solzhenitsyn he utilised brutal methods without compunction: 'We have to squeeze everything out of a prisoner in the first three months – after that we don't need him anymore.' In 1937 he became head of BAMLag (the Baikal Amur Mainline railway camp) and was Chief Directorate of Railroad Construction until 1945. He was awarded the Order of Lenin three times and made a Hero of Socialist Labour.

КРЕМЛЕВСКИЕ ПОДОПЫТНЫЕ „КРОЛИКИ"

По указанию Л.П.Берии в конце 30-х и 40-х годов приговоренных к расстрелу „врагов народа" мужчин и женщин разного возраста использовали в г.Москве и г. Шиханы для лабораторных опытов по применению „БОВ" (боевых отравляющих веществ).

The Kremlin's guinea pigs.

In the 1930s and 1940s, by order of Lavrenty Beria,[*] men and women 'enemies of the people' of all ages, who had been sentenced to death, were used for testing chemical weapons in laboratories in Moscow and Shikhany.

[*] Lavrentiy Beria was made head of the NKVD in 1938, where he oversaw the deportation of thousands to the Gulag from Poland and the Baltic states, following Soviet occupation of these countries. He mobilised the free labour offered by the camps to produce weapons during the Second World War, and after the war was responsible for the direct 'repatriation' to the Gulag of many Soviet soldiers. When Stalin died in 1953 he was made First Deputy Prime Minister, but was quickly denounced and executed by his political rivals.

193

ЛИКВИДАЦИЯ ЗАКЛЮЧЁННЫХ УПРАВЛЕНИЕМ ФИЗИЧЕСКОГО УНИЧТОЖЕНИЯ (УФУ) НКВД СССР

УФУ БЫЛО СФОРМИРОВАННО ВЗАМЕН ЧОН (ЧАСТИ ОСОБОГО НАЗНАЧЕНИЯ ВЧК-ГПУ, Т.Е. КАРАТЕЛЬНЫЕ) И ЗАНИМАЛОСЬ „СОКРАЩЕНИЕМ" ЗЭКОВ ГУЛАГа НКВД - БОЛЬНЫХ, ДИСТРОФИКОВ, ОТКАЗЧИКОВ И Т.Д. НА СЕВЕРЕ ПОСЛЕ МАССОВЫХ РАССТРЕЛОВ ТРУПЫ ЗЭКОВ ТОПИЛИ В БОЛОТАХ - „ЗЫБУНАХ" ИЛИ ЗАРЫВАЛИ В ВЕЧНУЮ МЕРЗЛОТУ „АММОНАЛЬНИКИ" ТАКЖЕ УФУ ИСПОЛНЯЛО ВМН (ВЫСШУЮ МЕРУ НАКАЗАНИЯ) ПО ПРИГОВОРАМ ТРОЕК, ОСОБЫХ СОВЕЩАНИЙ И Т.Д.

The liquidation of prisoners by the Department of Physical Extermination (UFU) of the USSR's NKVD.

The UFU replaced ChONs (Specialised Units of the VChK GPU, i.e. punitive) and was in the business of 'reducing' the number of prisoners of the Gulag prisons via execution by firing squad of the sick, weak, those who refused to work, and so on. In the north of the USSR, the bodies of the executed were thrown into swamps or buried in *ammonalniks** in the permafrost. The UFU also carried out capital punishment according to sentences handed down by the NKVD Troikas, special meetings, etc.

* See page 93.

По приказу „ОТЦА ВСЕХ НАРОДОВ" И.СТАЛИНА...

1940г. РАССТРЕЛ ПОЛЬСКИХ ОФИЦЕРОВ В ЛЕСАХ КАТЫНИ. КОММУНИСТЫ ПОСЛЕ ЗАХВАТА ВЛАСТИ В 1917г. ВБЛИЗИ ОБЛАСТНЫХ И КРУПНЫХ ГОРОДОВ ОТГОРОДИЛИ ТЕРРИТОРИИ ДЛЯ МАССОВЫХ КАЗНЕЙ „КЛАССОВЫХ ВРАГОВ": ПОД ЛЕНИНГРАДОМ - ЛЕВАШОВСКАЯ ПУСТОШЬ, г. ТОМСКОМ - КОЛПАШЕВО, г. СМОЛЕНСКОМ - КАТЫНЬ И Т.Д. И Т.П.

By order of the 'father of all peoples', Joseph Stalin.

1940. The execution of Polish officers at Katyn Forest.* After coming to power in 1917, the Communists reserved special territories around large cities and regional centres for mass executions of 'class enemies': Levashovskaya Pustosh near Leningrad, Kolpashevo near Tomsk, Katyn near Smolensk and so on.

* Between April and May of 1940, approximately 22,000 Polish nationals (including 8,000 Polish officers) were executed in what is now called the Katyn Massacre. In 1943 the German army found 4,243 bodies buried in a mass grave and attempted to use this discovery to split the allies. Stalin responded to these accusations by claiming that the Germans had committed the crime. The Soviet Union denied responsibility until 1990.

Будни ГУЛАГА Любимое детище партокра

После очередного отстрела „врагов наро,

По приказу министра МВД СССР Маршала Л.П.Берия расстрелянные, а такж
протыкались штыком в сердце, и головы дырявились контрольными выс

ПУ-НКВД ТАЛАНТЛИВЫЙ УЧИТЕЛЬ ГЕСТАПО И ВОЙСК СС...
ТОМАТОВ В КОЛЫМСКИХ ЛАГЕРЯХ ГУЛАГА...

И, С ЦЕЛЬЮ „ПРОФИЛАКТИКИ,"ЧТОБЫ „ЖИВОЙ" НЕ ПРИТВОРЯЛСЯ МЁРТВЫМ,"
ЫМ СОСТАВОМ УФУ (УПРАВЛЕНИЕ ФИЗИЧЕСКОГО УНИЧТОЖЕНИЯ) НКВД СССР...

Daily life of the Gulag. The favourite child of the party bureaucracy, the VChK, GPU, and NKVD, gifted mentor of the Gestapo and the SS.
After an execution of 'enemies of the people' by the firing squad in the Kolyma Gulag prison camps.

By order of the Minister of the MVD of the USSR, Marshal Lavrenty Beria,[*] as a 'preventive measure', prisoners who were executed or died of natural causes were stabbed in the heart with a bayonet and shot in the head by the UFU of the NKVD. This was done so that 'the living did not pretend to be dead'.

The Settling of Scores Inside Camps

Razborki (the settling of scores) took place among Gulag prisoners for any number of reasons: to gain easier labour; for better clothes or footwear; for a better seat in the canteen or at an event in the camp; for a better bunk; or for reasons of an 'ideological' nature. These violent *razborki* were often initiated by criminals belonging to the 'suit' (caste) of thieves, who claim leadership among the prisoners, and always considered themselves as having the highest status in the camp hierarchy. Scores were settled through fights, the infliction of severe injuries and killings.

Following the abolition of the death penalty for murder in the Supreme Council of the USSR's decree of 26th May 1947, there was a dramatic escalation of *razborki* within the camps. The most hardened thieves who had no hope of release (those serving sentences of twenty-five years or more), took to murdering *bytoviks* (prisoners who had committed crimes but were not part of the criminal world); knowing they'd be sent away for five or six months 'rest' to an investigatory prison while the killing was looked into (those under investigation were better fed).

I met many of these 'murderers on holiday' at various prisons: Khabarovsk, Chita, Ulan-Ude, Irkutsk, Taishet and Krasnoyarsk. They were happy with their situation, even smiling and bragging about it, *'Nachal'nik* (chief), I don't care, I have twenty-five years in front of me. Fuck it, I'll hang around here for five or six months, then after the trial I'll go back to my *zona* (camp or prison) or another one. I'll kill any *fraer* ('outsider') if it's necessary. It's as easy as getting my fingers wet when I piss.' For this type of heavyweight criminal, killing a person meant nothing – this was the scum that the Communists were attempting to change. The decrees of 4th June 1947 made crimes concerning 'protection of a citizen's personal property' and 'theft of state and common property' carry a mandatory twenty or twenty-five year sentence. *Razborki* quickly became extremely bloody and merciless, as convicted criminals had little left to lose.

These decrees split the criminal world into two irreconcilable camps. To survive in Gulag conditions with such long sentences some criminals from the 'thieves suit' began to collaborate with the camp's administration, taking trusted positions inside the camp. They became stock keepers in clothing, footwear and vegetable warehouses; took jobs as blacksmiths, drivers, librarians – anything to prevent them from being sent to work at the hard labour sites, where mining, logging and heavy construction work meant life expectancy was short.

The other part of the 'thieves suit' continued their customary conflict with the administration. Ignoring the camp rules they refused to work to produce the norm required by the plan, and they were duly punished. According to the thieves' law they must not work, or be obliged to work, but live only by criminal means. This elite, 'ideological' group of thieves began calling the other group (those who cooperated with the administration, abandoning the thieves' law) 'bitches'. Over the years the number of 'bitches' grew as their work for the administration allowed them to survive, but their characters didn't change – they were still society's parasites, who continued to commit robberies, murders and other crimes.

The prison and camp authorities were keen to reduce the quantity of inmates. To this end they would deliberately place criminals of opposite 'suits' together in the same cell. Packed with two or three times more inmates than they could hold, the fighting in these common cells was fatal. Once the administration decided there were enough dead and seriously injured, they would intervene, taking the bodies to the mortuary and the wounded to the prison hospital.

In the 1950s I witnessed the results of these clashes in transition prisons in Suchan (renamed Arseniev), Irkutsk, Krasnoyarsk, Omsk and Kirov (Viatka). These wars between 'ideological' thieves and 'bitches' were led by 'commanders' on both sides. The fights in the camp zones of the Khabarovsky region, Irkutsky region, Bratsky region (where the hydropower plants were built), Krasnoyarsk region and the Norilsk region, regularly resulted in up to a hundred injured or dead.

When groups of prisoners were transported in lorries, rail carriages or by foot, the guards always separated thieves from 'bitches', while other types of criminals, including the political prisoners, remained neutral during these 'wars'. The situation was the same inside the camps. When a new group of prisoners arrived, they were immediately lined up outside and separated: one of the administration's seniors would shout, 'Thieves to the right! Bitches to the left! *Muzhiks, fraers* stay were you are!' Then they would be taken to the separate barracks according to their 'suits'. 'Local fencing' constructed from barbed wire usually separated their respective areas within the camp. During this exceptionally cruel period, if a thief or a 'bitch' happened to find himself in the barrack of the wrong 'suit', it always meant *kranty* (death).

The fights, injuries and deaths caused by these warring factions became a huge hindrance, preventing camps from achieving the norm required by the plan – which was of paramount importance to the administration. In particular the 'thieves in law' (legitimate thieves) and their minions were a real obstruction. Many senior camp chiefs complained to the heads of the Gulag and MVD, pointing out the growing numbers of thieves 'in authority' who refused to work, while the plan quotas continued to be based simply on the number of prisoners a camp held. To this effect the MVD Minister Beria, with the agreement from the CPSU Central Committee's Politburo, took the decision to liquidate the 'thieves in law' and their associates. He issued an order to move them to seven camps in the Sverdlovsk (Ekaterinburg) region, which had been specially formed in 1949. The camp chiefs did this with great relief.

When I worked in Leningrad prison No. 1: 'Kresty', two of my fellow guards, Vanya Mikhailov and Sasha Fiodorov, told me the following story about their time at these camps. In early summer 1949 they were sent to Sverdlovsk, where they guarded a camp from high observation towers. They were told it contained especially dangerous thieves and criminal 'authorities' who had been imprisoned there to help them correct their ways.

They later found out that all seven camps held between 20,000 to 25,000 prisoners, brought from various regions of the USSR. This particular camp did not have a production zone like other camps, so the prisoners did not work. While Mikhailov and Fiodorov were there another 300 or 400 prisoners were brought in, making a total of around 3,500 in their camp. Inevitably, the 'score settling' started – mass fights began for leadership of the camp. Criminals from Sverdlovsk attacked those from Chelyabinsk, while criminals from Irkutsk attacked those from Vorkuta; there were fights between Khabarovsk and Omsk, Krasnoyark and Mordova, Kolyma and Moscow, Kiev and Kazan, Tashkent and Novosibirk. They started in the barracks, then spread to two canteen buildings. Day and night the fights raged, becoming increasingly violent until they reached massacre proportions. Prisoners were chasing each other with any kind of weapon they could find: bricks, iron bars, even wooden planks torn from their bunks.

A special team from a neighbouring camp consisting of forty or so *muzhiks-bytoviks* (everyday criminals) with short sentences, were brought in to load the dead onto lorries. The wounded were ignored. The criminals didn't stop, every day they continued to kill one another. All this could clearly be seen from the observation towers, but the camp administration did nothing. One night the prisoners started a fire in the canteen, they burnt their barracks, and then a food depot. The fire brigade were not called.

The starvation began in the camp zone. Any food remaining after the depot had been burned soon ran out. It was then that the thieves began to eat each other, larger groups chasing smaller ones, as if they were hunting. They gathered pieces of scrap wood and boiled the human flesh in any saucepan they could find that had survived the fire. Many criminals died of wounds, injuries and starvation. About 100 were ultimately saved from death by the camp's chief administration.

Those who buried the dead were disgusted as they handled the half eaten bodies with muscles cut out. Through November and December of 1949 the rest of the frozen corpses of the 'thieves in law' were removed. They had been the second 'shadow' authority in the camps, preventing the other prisoners from completing their quotas because of their 'score settling'. The 'bitches' were not eliminated, they had found common ground with the administration, working to complete the plan, while saving themselves at the same time. The dead were buried in mass graves in the camp cemeteries, their bodies covered with chlorine lime for sanitation reasons.

The typical cause of death on any coroner's report from a Gulag camp was either heart or kidney failure. This standard diagnosis covered every eventuality, for example: if the inmate had been killed in a fight; during a beating; while attempting to escape; or if they were political prisoners killed on the orders of the NKVD-MGB or by an in-camp criminal 'authority'.

NKVD-MVD instructions demanded that every corpse be labelled before it left the mortuary. The prisoner's camp number was written in soft pencil on a six by eight centimetre label of thick cardboard, which was then attached by cord or wire to the big toe of each body. This process was undertaken in case of future exhumation, the pencil graphite kept well in damp soil.

The same NKVD-MVD instruction obliged the guards at the camp checkpoint to 'hole-punch' the dead before releasing them from the zone. A sharpened hammer was used to pierce the skulls and chests of the bodies. Only after a corpse had been punched could it be registered in the camp journal. Some time ago the leader of the world proletariat claimed that 'Accounting and control is the essence of socialist transformation', [Lenin 1929] while the Gulag inmates used to say, 'They hole-punch our brains so the dead prisoner doesn't think he's still alive'.

MVD Minister Lavrenty Beria had a good grasp of psychology, he knew the mentality of the criminal 'authorities' and 'legitimate' thieves: their self-centred nature, their naked lust for leadership that manifested itself in this display of inconceivable cruelty. His calculation that these rivals would tear each other apart was deadly accurate. Following this unprecedented incident people believed the criminal world was capable of destroying itself, if the right conditions were created for it to happen. This was proven in the Sverdlovsk camps; Beria's initiative struck a serious blow to the criminal world.

A Comparison of Communist Party and Criminal Power Structures

I spent thirty-three years working for the NKVD (People's Commissariat for Internal Affairs), the MVD (Ministry of Internal Affairs) and the Bureau of Criminal Investigation of the GUVD (State Directorate for Internal Affairs), retiring in July 1981. As a former employee of these law-enforcement authorities, I have always been interested in the connection between the ideology of the criminal world and our socialist society, and would like to share my thoughts and observations.

In February 1967 I visited Ivan Belyaev, an old army friend of mine who lived in Irkutsk. Here I met a distant relative of his wife's – a *vor v zakone* (thief in law) Golovin, alias Golova (Head), who was about twenty years older than me. At that time, Golova was still a sturdy old man of square build, medium height, rather well-groomed, with a round head and greying hair. I could see well-drawn tattoos of thieves' symbols on his wrists. This old and experienced 'thief in law' had spent thirty-one years – almost half of his life, in places of detention.

Golova's language was full of words and expressions from thieves' jargon. I spent four days talking to him and taking notes. He was born in a big village called Aleksandrovskoe, home to the Aleksandrovskaya Central Hard-Labour Prison, well-known all over Siberia, situated about thirty kilometres from Irkutsk.

As he talked about his village, he sang me a verse from a song which I'd first heard at the October Revolution Orphanage for Family Members of Traitors of the Motherland, where I was placed after my father, Sergei Petrovich Baldaev, a veteran scholar-folklore specialist and ethnographer had been arrested:

Far away in Irkutsk land
Between two gigantic cliffs
Aleksandrovsky Central
Lies behind high wall of bricks

Tens of thousands of 'class enemies' were eliminated in Aleksandrovsky Central, and their corpses buried in the forest a short distance from this gloomy establishment. Golova told me that in czarist days his father had served a sentence there for horse-stealing. He was released under surveillance and married a girl from the neighbouring village of Khomutovo. Before 1917 Golova's father found him a job as a stonemason, but after meeting the local thieves, Golova quit work and stepped onto the criminal path. He took pride in being a thief by birth and becoming a 'thief in law', which meant that he didn't work in prison. He was a *pakhan* (criminal boss) in the camps of Siberia, Primorie and Kolyma. Although he'd had no academic education, he was quite a well-read person, gifted by nature, with an original, sharp mind and vivid interest in the country's political life. At his house I saw a small library and various newspapers and magazines: *Pravda*, *The Atheist*, *Health Magazine*, *Krestyanka* (*Peasant Woman*), *Political Self-Education*, etc. He explained to me that his passion for reading had developed in the Gulag camps.

Golova spoke with a certain pride, even bravado, about the authorities of Dalstroy and other camps and their deferential and respectful attitude toward 'thieves in law' (legitimate thieves); let alone toward the camps' *pakhans* who, after the administration, were practically the zone's masters. According to him the legitimate thieves were an invaluable help in the completion and over-completion of the Gulag's production plans. They made 'hanger-backs', *muzhiks* and *frayer-kontriks* (political prisoners), work as much as the authorities needed and at any time – even when the temperature was sixty below.

The *bugry* (top men) in the camps were usually the criminals. They did no work themselves, but made the other convicts work by threatening their health and lives.

Golova knew I worked for the authorities, and he liked that I was a keen listener. During our conversations he questioned his own past, and I could feel that this old offender was depressed by his lonely life. Listed below are the 'philosophical' conclusions that he had come to about the hierarchy in the criminal world. To him I represented the authorities and was a member of the Communist Party, so he often used the words 'you' and 'us':

1. In the 'big zone' (the Soviet Union), you have the general secretary, the most important *pakhan* (criminal boss) – head of the socialist camp and of the Politburo of the Central Committee of the Communist Party of the Soviet Union, which consists of very big *pakhans*. They all get help upholding their 'suit' (power) from MVD, MGB (Ministry of State Security) and the army. Everyone is scared of them, and if anyone steps out of line – he'll be put against the wall. They can imprison or kill a hundred million people, and nobody will object or dare say a word.

In our 'small zone' (the camp) we also have our main camp *pakhan* from the 'first five', these 'first five' are like your Politburo. None of the prisoners will ever dare say anything to them, and those who dissent will immediately be brutally beaten or killed by the thieves 'suit' in the prison, whether it's two or three brigades or half a barrack.

2. You have your Central Committee, the *pakhans* reporting to Politburo and its Secretary General. Our version of this are the *urki* (authoritative 'legitimate' thieves), who are not in the 'first five' *pakhans*.

3. You have the Supreme Council. We thieves, have this kind of 'council' too. It consists of *kodly* (less authoritative thieves) who report to the *pakhans*.

4. Then you have your Council of Ministers. We have the same type of 'council of ministers' consisting of *khevra* (even less authoritative thieves) who hold the positions of *bugry* (gang leaders) in the working brigades of convicts.

5. Your Communist Party organises congresses and assemblies, where different resolutions are discussed and various decisions are made. We thieves discuss our business at *pakhans* meetings in Moscow, Leningrad and Tashkent, and 'assemblies' of 'thieves in law' in camps and colonies.

6. Your Secretary General and members of the Politburo have their bodyguards. Our 'big *pakhans*' have their 'flunkies' (thieves' guards and skivvies).

7. Your Communist Party (apart from grass roots) makes the workers, farmers and intelligentsia work their arses off for them. We, 'thieves in law', also make 'thieves' *muzhiks*' (convicts who give away a certain percentage of their proceeds to thieves) and other prisoners in the zone work for us.

8. Your Communist Party (apart from grass roots) takes away from workers and farmers everything they produce. We 'thieves in law', also take away from prisoners in camps: clothes, shoes, food parcels, anything we like.

9. Your Communist Party (apart from grass roots) taxes the intelligentsia, the workers, and the farmers. We, the camp's *pakhans*, also make the working brigades pay the 'Abyssinian tax' [a 'protection' payment].

10. Your Communist Party (apart from grass roots), after taking away everything the workers have produced, distribute it how they like. We, 'thieves in law', after taking away the prisoners nice clothes, shoes and food parcels, distribute them how we like.

11. You call your people 'members of the Communist Party'. We call thieves *blatnye*.

12. Your Communist Party has its own regulations. We, ('committed') thieves, have our 'thieves' law' (not many people are aware of it, even if they work for law-enforcement authorities). These are its rules:

a) to estrange oneself from one's family – mother, father, sisters and brothers.

b) it is forbidden to have a family of one's own (no wife, no children), but only to have mistresses – they should have names like: 'barukha', 'biksa', 'dyrka' (a hole), 'marukha', 'prostiachka' (a simpleton), 'soska' ([cock]sucker), 'shalashovka', 'shkura' (a pelt), etc.

c) it is forbidden to work anywhere, you may only live from the proceeds of a life of crime.

Golova has known this 'thieves' law' since before the 1917 October Revolution, and 'raised' many young thieves to follow these rules.

13. Golova also told me how both outside and inside the camp, *pakhans* send their 'flunkies' to the 'cunning little house' (Police Operational Unit) to find out what the authorities' plans are, and the identities of moles in prisons and police departments.

14. He also told me about the existence of the thieves' secret mail (similar to the Communist Party government top secret post), which is used to deliver information on prisoner transport, moles and secret orders around the Gulag, etc.

Golova compared the thieves 'communal' money box to the beneficial association of the Trade Union and the Communist Party; and thieves' 'sons' and 'kids' to pioneers and members of the Komsomol (Communist Youth Organisation). He insisted that Communist Party jargon was very similar to the thieves jargon known as *fenia*. Flipping through the pages of the *Political Self-Education* magazine, he called this once-popular Communist Party publication a 'Political Self-Besotter'. He boiled over at the stupidity of regular citizens, who at their meetings, rallies and lectures parroted the 'shit' peddled by the Communist Party *pakhans*. He took pleasure in telling me how prisoners brutalised political officers from the camp's Cultural and Educational Unit during their political lectures. He then continued:

15. You have regional, territorial and provincial committees in your 'big zone', the ones that hold the local power. In our 'small zone' we thieves have those who hold the 'suit' (power) in residential barracks, prisoners' brigades, units, industrial territories, canteens, warehouses, hospitals, etc. In the camp the thieves' categories are: 'centre', 'trump' and 'cool'. All the prisoners are scared of them, and not a single *muzhik* or *kontrik* (political prisoner) will ever dare to go against them.

16. Your Communist Party consists of lower sections: Communist Party groups, bureaus, committees. We thieves have something similar: 'thieves' families' consisting of *polozhnyaki* (middle ranking thieves), *v predelakh* (a thief with authority within the 'family'), *khavalshiki* (gullible ones) and *shesterkas* (literally 'sixes': flunkies).

17. You, the Communists, have your prosecutor's office, people's court, MVD, MGB, i.e. your punitive state agencies. Within the camp we have such 'agencies' too: *betushnye* (thieves who know the 'thieves' law' well, and who have never broken it) are our prosecutors and judges at *skhodnyaki* (assemblies), the *bespredely* (those without order, lawless) and *gulivany* (heads) are our MGB, the *boytsy* (blokes) and *borzye* (greyhounds) punish prisoners for not obeying the *betushnye* ('honest' thieves) or not respecting decisions made at the 'assemblies', or simply when they feel like it. We also have our executors of capital punishment – the *mochily* (assassins). When they receive an order

from the camp's *pakhan*, they will kill anyone, from ordinary prisoners to a superintendent or supervisor.

According to Golova, the only 'service' lacking in prison is a special unit like that of the MGB which hires girls from the age of eighteen. He found out about this practise from a former MGB employee named Krasik. Krasik told him about his work at the MGB, where they select girls discerningly, like at a ballet school. The candidate must be beautiful and slim. They measure her hips, waist and bust according to specific standards, and then she undergoes a strict medical check-up. The Operational Units of MGB meticulously check her political loyalty, close and distant relatives, friends, acquaintances and Komsomol references. Then the candidate for these 'special services' is made to sign a confidentiality agreement (about non-disclosure of State secrets). After all this, the girl is sent to a special institution outside Moscow. Here she is taught the basics of working for the Intelligence Services, as well as a comprehensive course in sexual practises. After completing their training, these girls become state prostitutes with decent salaries and special benefits.

They 'serve' the *pakhans* of the Communist Party during their revelries at the closed and strictly guarded dachas. The 'state sluts', who are under secret instructions, don't know each other. All these girls have 'cover papers' saying that they are employed by scientific institutions, etc. They are rarely 'uncovered', even their families will have no idea what kind of 'special state service' their daughter is engaged in. According to the 'agreement', these women have no right to marry until they are thirty-five years old. When they reach that age, they 'retire' and live off a pension. If the 'slut' has completed her working period from the age of eighteen until she is thirty-five, she can be transferred to other services in the armed units of the Communist Party.

I asked Golova how Krasik was so familiar with these 'special state services'. He replied, 'The former MGB employee Krasik had worked for a few years as a guard at the house of one such Communist Party rat, who'd 'retired' and was working at the regional committee of the *pakhan* party.'

18. You have stars, medals, different badges. We don't wear this kind of bauble unless we're on a job where we need this masquerade. But we also have our marks of distinction – tattoos, and everyone must 'answer' to the thieves for his tattoos. For example, none of the *muzhiks*, *fraers* (dummies, outsiders) and other non-thieves has the right to wear the following tattoos: a cross, a church or a monastery with domes and crosses, an eagle, a lion, a tiger, Jesus Christ, archangels, Saints, Our Lady, angels, czarist heraldry, or a skull (a symbol of fearlessness and loyalty to 'thieves' laws'). Sometimes a non-thief, outsider with 'self-appointed' tattoos ends up in prison. He will first be asked by the thieves whether he can answer for his tattoos. If he can't, he'll be beaten up, and then made to remove the tattoos using sandpaper, glass, a knife or another sharp item.

19. You have the so-called political officers. In the Gulag camps they are called 'priests', 'shamans', *fuflogons* (rubbish-talkers) and are supposed to preach to us thieves and other prisoners. We also have those who teach young thieves our 'thieves' laws' and 'rules'. They are the old 'thieves in law'.

20. Different non-party people support and believe in your Communist Party. We, thieves, also have our non-*blatnye* who have a fellow feeling for us: 'kenty' (mates), *kiriukhi* (fellow countrymen).

21. You expel members from the Communist Party for different misdeeds. We make decisions at the 'assembly' to relegate certain 'thieves in law'. We call ours *yershi* (ruff fish), you call yours *lishenets partbileta* (bereft of party membership).

22. In your Communist Party, Politburo or Central Committee, there is often an ideological fight between the top *pakhans* of the Party. In the camps we also have this kind of fight among our thieves' *pakhans*. Thieves transferred from Moscow, Leningrad, Sverdlovsk, Novosibirsk, Krasnoyarsk or from Irkutsk, all have their own *pakhans* who kill one another fighting for power – *krutiat kranty* (to the death). I remember how in Kraslag, Tayshetlag and in the Kolyma camps you could end up with thirty, fifty or even a hundred *zhmuriki* (dead bodies) in two days. Us 'thieves in law', fight over power exactly like you do in your Communist Party.

23. In all their years of power, the Communists have always had 'class enemies' whom they would shoot incessantly. We 'thieves in law' have also always had our enemies – *suki* (bitches: those who'd stepped away from 'thieves' laws' and 'rules'). We showed them no mercy.

24. Prisoners in camps used to be divided into three 'suits': thieves, *muzhiks* and *suki*. The thieves and the *suki* were in a deadly feud with each another. *Suki* detached themselves from *ideynye* (committed) thieves after a new decree had been issued by the PVS (Presidium of the Supreme Soviet) of the USSR on the 4th June 1947, stating new sentences of up to twenty-five years. To survive in the Gulags, they would work for the camp administration, never clashing with them, unlike *ideynye* thieves. Often they landed good jobs, working as aides in medical units, stock keepers, etc. Sometimes the thieves zone would attack the *suki* zone, and vice versa. If a thief accidentally found himself in the zone or cell of the *suki*, that would be the end of him, and of course, a *suka* would be killed in the thieves' zone or cell. Everything is just as you have it in your Communist Party when it comes to the 'class struggle'.

25. According to Golova, the whole society of the Soviet Union resembles a woodpile. There are those who are on the top, others in the middle and some at the very bottom. The ones at the top are the main *pakhans* – the Secretary General, the members of the Politburo of the Communist Party Central Committee. Below them are the Ministries *pakhans*, lower still are all the regional, territorial, city and area committees' *pakhans*. Gulag prisoners hold exactly the same positions in their environment.

This old recidivist, a 'thief in law', said that he'd done a lot of thinking and had come to the conclusion that the two power structures were identical, the Communist Party in 'the big zone' and the thieves in 'the small zone'. He was convinced that if he had studied more when he was young, he would have become a big *pakhan* in the Party. He would be eating Communist Party food, and living in a luxurious, expensively furnished city apartment, with a dacha in an idyllic place, complete with domestic workers and guards. Just like the *pakhans* from the Irkutsk Regional Committee – he considered himself to be no worse than them.

Forms of Humiliation, Torture and Murder Practised in the Gulag

Bantik-krantik (*bantik* 'bow tie' and *krantik* diminutive of *kranty* 'finished, done in')
The strangulation of a victim with a towel at night.

Vecherniy zvon lokham (vesper chimes for dupes)
Following roll-call, after the guards had locked the barrack doors, the oppressed prisoners of the camp would be battered by the privileged criminals. The battering is a form of punishment for various offenses, carried out by the *otritsalovka* (literally 'deniers') – the most aggressive group of thieves.

V lyagushku sazhat (to do the frog)
A form of torture whereby the victim is made to sit on the floor with his arms and legs stuck in the sleeves of a jacket, and the back of the jacket flipped over his head. The victim is then kicked or beaten with a heavy object across the back and head.

Vylozhenny, vykholoshchenny rusak (gelded *rusak* 'Russophile')
A convict who has been castrated at night in the barracks as a punishment for the murder of a person of Asian descent by the compatriots of the murdered. After castration, the perpetrators do not kill the victim for moral reasons, or for fear their sentences will be prolonged, or even for fear of execution by the authorities. The administration never made these cases public. The culprits were put in isolation cells and the victim was hospitalised. If the victim died, it was written off with a 'standard' cause of death: renal failure, heart attack, etc.

Dat petukhu pendelya (to kick a rooster)
For breaching thieves' and prison law, it is customary to kick the outcasts (the lowest rank of prisoners). The thieves' law forbids touching the outcast so as not to be defiled.

Zhit sovdepu/sovku vredno! (life's no bed of roses for a *sovok*! *Sovok* is a derogatory term for a person with a Soviet mentality)
A phrase uttered to a newly arrived inmate as a warning before beating takes place for a breach of thieves' and prison laws, rules and etiquette.

Zagnat mokhnorylogo petukha v sortir (to lock a *mokhnoryly* – literally 'cunt-face' – rooster in the outhouse; *mokhnoryly* is a base criminal, usually a rapist)
A prisoner who was sentenced for child molesting would be locked up in an outhouse for the entire work day. Other prisoners would then sodomise the victim or force him to perform oral sex. Usually the *mokhnoryly* would commit suicide after such humiliations.

Zadelat turetsky shashlyk (to make a Turkish kebab)
1. The impalement by privileged prisoners of an informer on a pike or a crowbar hammered into ground (or frozen into it). 2. The impalement of a political prisoner with the consent of the prison authorities as a form of deterrent for other political prisoners.

Zadrochke raskovyryat tselku (to pop a slut's cherry)
Group defloration in a female prison for minors of a scorned victim, performed by authoritative inmates by pushing a toothbrush case, a spoon, etc. into the vagina.

Za nakolki otvechaesh? (can you vouch for your tattoos?)
A question addressed by authoritative prisoners to newly arrived inmates. Each prisoner is responsible for his tattoos, because they must represent his true position in the criminal hierarchy. If any of his tattoos do not correspond to his rank, he is forced – under penalty of severe torture or death – to remove them with a knife, sandpaper, or a piece of glass. Refusals result in the most severe battering for imposture.

Zapodolit govnoedku (to shame the shit-eater)

A widespread form of humiliation for shunned prisoners in female prisons for minors. The victim's skirt is pulled up and tied over her head. Then her underpants are taken off and the victim is seated in snow, a puddle, mud, or a plot of stinging nettles.

Zaryadit kankan za zapadlo (to dance a cancan for breaching [the thieves' law])
A heinous form of execution carried out by authoritative prisoners, widespread in northern Gulag prison camps. The victim is stripped naked and his feet are cut off. Then they are forced to dance, while the perpetrators poke him with knives and crowbars which have been heated up in the barracks stove. The execution ends when the victim falls on the floor and a crowbar is inserted two feet deep, into his anus. Sometimes the crowbar is inserted deeper, until it appears at the throat.

Za svoi slova otvechaesh? (can you back that up?)
A question addressed to a prisoner by the inmates. According to the thieves' law, a prisoner must answer to the authoritative criminals for every word or phrase he says. In remote northern prison camps, where idle talk is inadmissible, serious injuries or even murders can occur as a result of a rash insult. Because of this law convicts from the south or west of Russia, including many so-called tough racketeers, are mortally afraid of ending up in a northern or Siberian prison.

Zakhotel letet, perdet i kakat? (feel like flying, farting, and shitting?)
A warning to an underage victim by low-life or lumpen peers in specialised prisons for juveniles before a cruel punishment. The punishment involves beating up the victim, shoving him inside a bedside cupboard, and throwing it out of a window or off the roof of a building. The perpetrators then rush to observe the outcome of their execution.

Zashvabrit lokha/fraera (to broomstick a *lokh/fraer*; *lokh* or *fraer* 'uninitiated outsider')
By an order of authoritative criminals, as a punishment for an offence, the handle of a broom or mop is inserted into the anus to a depth of up to ten inches. The other end is tied to the victim's feet, preventing him or her from getting up from the floor. This torture was widespread in Gulag prisons for both men and women. Such cruel tortures were never used in hard labour prisons during the 'cursed czarist regime'.

Indijsky krant (the Indian *krant*; from *kranty* 'finished, done in')
A form of execution of a criminal using a hacksaw, by direct order of an authoritative criminal, or as a result of a criminal council.

Karandash zasunut (to stick a pencil up)
An execution of a criminal by inserting a crowbar, or the stick of a broom or mop, into the anus to a depth of up to two feet by direct order of an authoritative criminal, as a result of a criminal council, or by order of prison authorities (against political prisoners). This form of torture became widespread in the Gulag prisons after the decree of the Presidium of the Supreme Council of the USSR of 26th May 1947, which abolished the death penalty for murder of one or more people.

Krugovoe poluchalovo (round robin beating up)
Mutual beating of inmates in a prison cell, ordered by an authoritative criminal as punishment; the manifestation of the 'one for all' principle (when everybody is responsible for one person's misdeeds). The misdeeds may include failure to overdo the labour quota, production of defective goods, slow work, etc. The authoritative criminal personally beats those who do not demonstrate enough enthusiasm in beating their fellow cellmates and kicks them with heavy boots, punches them, or hits them with a stick or a toilet plunger.

Lek s gemoglobinom i kvasom (a *lek* with hemoglobin and *kvas*; *lek* 'oral sex between women', *kvas* 'bread drink' made from black or rye bread)
A form of humiliation in prisons for women. Under the threat of a beating, an authoritative thief forces the shunned inmates (*zadrochkas, zadryuchkas, suchonkas*) to lick her menstrual blood.

Napyalit trusy na tykvu (to pull a pair of panties over the melon)
A form of punishment or entertainment whereby authoritative criminals in women's prisons put a pair of underpants on the head of a shunned inmate, then beat her with brooms or wet, twisted bed sheets, until she is covered in bruises.

Obmenyatsa kobylkami/korovkami/kurochkami/nevestami (to swap brides)
An exchange by authoritative female criminals, active lesbians, of their passive partners for a few sessions of intercourse. As a token of friendship, authoritative thieves exchange their passive lesbian partners like slaves for a short time, or until either the active or the passive lesbian is discharged from prison. Afterwards passive lesbians are often unwilling to live with a man, as they believe that only a woman can properly satisfy another woman.

Obmenyatsa petukhami (to swap roosters)
As a token of friendship, criminals in prisons exchange their passive homosexual partners with other privileged, active homosexuals. Natural passive homosexuals are particularly valuable, due to their appealing feminine physique and 'woman's soul'.

Oserebrit (to silver-plate someone)
A punishment whereby mercury from two or three broken thermometers, stolen from the prison hospital, is forced down the throat of an offending criminal. A long, drawn-out death, sometimes lasting for years, is inevitable.

Otmorozhenny, otmorozok podnarnik (lame-brained, moronic; also an extremist)
A convicted racketeer, a pawn and a goon. When out of prison, he prefers to wear a raspberry-coloured jacket and a long black overcoat. [These raspberry-coloured jackets are considered to be a uniform of the 'New Russians' who emerged after perestroika. Their lifestyle is generally characterised by bad taste and a love of ostentation. Outside the prison they have power and use it to get their own way, but inside they are mocked and humiliated.] He is not familiar with the thieves' law, rules, and etiquette. Because of his presumptuous behaviour and other misdeeds, he is beaten and becomes an outcast.

Otkhodit zadrochku skrutkoy (to beat up a slut with a twister)
Beating of a shunned female prisoner with a wet, twisted bed sheet.

Pechenku otbit (to beat the liver)
A form of punishment whereby the victim is kicked in the stomach area. The punishment is usually inflicted for disobeying the *pakhan* (an authoritative thief), for a breach of the thieves' law and rules, or for a denunciation. The NKVD, KGB, etc., also ordered common criminals to carry out such beatings on political prisoners.

Podarit/prodat svoego petukha (to give as a gift/sell one's rooster)
In the Gulag prison system, an authoritative *pakhan* who kept several passive homosexuals as a harem could sell or give one or two of them as a gift to another authoritative *pakhan*, or exchange them for an object that caught his fancy.

Poimet vetochku (to get a twig)
A sadistic card game in which the winner cuts off the loser's finger or toe (usually the little finger or toe, depending on their preliminary agreement), in the presence of other

prisoners as witnesses.

Poimet pelmen (to get a dumpling)

To win an ear or both ears, cutting them off the loser in front of other prisoners who act as witnesses. The wounds are usually powdered with hot ashes from the barracks stove.

Poimet faru (to get a headlamp)

A sadistic card game, in which the winner carves out the loser's eye with a knife or pulls it out with his fingers in the presence of other prisoners as witnesses. Usually, prisoners who have lost everything, including their clothing, will bet one of their eyes. The eye is then placed on the table for everyone to see. Criminals use such cruel games to demonstrate their strength of spirit, their mercilessness and the sacredness of debt in card games in the criminal world.

Prikryt myakotyu dykh (to cover one's throat with flesh)

To strangle an unwanted prisoner by direct order of an authoritative criminal or as a result of a criminal council. The victim's mouth and nose are covered with a palm, while other prisoners hold the victim's arms and legs. This method was also used for murdering political prisoners. They were then written off with a 'standard' cause of death: renal failure, stroke, etc.

Progret trebukhu (to warm up the intestines)

An extreme form of execution reserved for delinquent prisoners in the Gulag, whereby the victim is forced onto his hands and knees and a red-hot crowbar is inserted into his rectum, while the criminals (the *pakhan*'s minions) hold him down.

Ptichka-khimichka priletnaya (a 'chemist' homing pigeon)

A convicted woman who has escaped from a construction site for fear of being raped, mugged, or beaten by male ex-convicts ('chemists'). She then chooses to return to the woman's prison to finish her term, even though she had been on parole for good behaviour or over-fulfilling the quota.

Razbit faneru (to crack the plywood)

Breaking the victim's chest with a hammer. This form of torture was often practised in juvenile prisons, where children of the lumpen proletariat would maim the shunned teenagers.

Saechki (literally 'bread rolls')

Methodical beatings of an out of favour convict in prison. The victim was hit, kicked, or punched in the stomach, liver, kidneys, solar plexus, head, or testicles. Also widespread in specialised institutions for difficult children and juvenile prisons, and practised by children of the lumpen proletariat.

Svoim petukhom ugostit (to treat someone to one's rooster)

In the Gulag prison system, an authoritative *pakhan* would offer his 'slave' – his personal (young and handsome) passive homosexual, as a token of friendship or respect, to any other privileged active homosexual for one or two sessions of intercourse.

Sdelat lastochku (to do a swallow)

To throw an out of favour prisoner from a top floor window by order of the *pakhan* or by mutual agreement of a group of criminals.

Sotvorit kosyak (to force a *kosyak* 'mistake')

1. To provoke (through deception) an out of favour prisoner to breach the thieves' law in prison. 2. To find compromising information in the biography of a non-authoritative

prisoner: membership in the Komsomol or Communist Party; service in the police forces; being a 'presser' in the 'press-hut' ['anti-social' convicts would be driven into 'pressing-huts', where the 'pressers' – specially selected criminals – 'applied the method of Leninist physical persuasion', beating and raping them until they were 'completely broken'. The 'pressers' were well-fed from other prisoners' food parcels and not made to do any work. If after his release a 'presser' offended again and ended up in a part of the zone where his former activities were known, his life was made a living hell. He would not usually survive for very long]; a passive homosexual; a record in a psychiatric institution; a former political prisoner; etc.

Sunut bolt, chtoby politzhopa poumnela (to stick a bolt in, in order to make a political arse smarter)
An act of forcible sodomy performed by common criminals by order of the NKVD. The victims were enemies of the people and contras who refused to work in a *sharashka*, or priests who refused to deny their faith. The common criminals were rewarded with food expropriated from parcels meant for other prisoners.

Taburetovka (from *taburetka* 'stool')
1. A form of sadism in prisons whereby an out of favour prisoner is hit around the head with a wooden stool or a small bench until he loses consciousness. 2. The same act performed on a political prisoner by an order of the NKVD.

Turetskaya svadba (Turkish wedding)
A savage reprisal against an informer in a women's prison. A shovel handle is inserted into the rectum or vagina up to two feet deep, damaging the internal organs and eventually killing the victim.

Turnut po mande/pizde meshalkoy (to shove in the cunt with a mixer; to put someone in his/her place)
A term used in women's prisons, referring to the expulsion of a privileged thief from a criminal group for not keeping up her promise to the authoritative thieves.

Ugostit svoej kurochkoy (to treat someone to one's own hen)
As a token of her positive predisposition, an active privileged lesbian offers her passive lesbian partner as a slave to another active authoritative lesbian for one or two sessions of intercourse. Passive lesbians must take care of and serve their active partners: launder clothes, make the bed, comb their hair, massage and bathe them, provide cigarettes, share food parcels, make or mend clothing. They must only partner their *kobla* (husband) during prison dances. Jealousy often caused cruel fights at such dances, and injuries were common. Both passive and active lesbians participated in these fights. On many occasions, after serving their sentences and getting out of prison, a passive lesbian would return to her husband or live with a man. Her former active lesbian partner, after being released herself, would then kill her former lover.

Ukontropupit v sortir/klozet (to drown in the outhouse)
To knock out a political prisoner, then drown him in the outhouse.

Fiksatsiya na shkonke (to affix to a bunk bed)
To punish an out of favour prisoner, on the orders of one of the prison's criminal authorities, by hanging them upside down with their hands tied.

Khimiki snoshayut i familiyu ne sprashivayut (the 'chemists' screw you and don't ask your name)

A common phrase used by convicted women who escaped from the settlement where they lived and worked while on parole. There they were gang-raped at night by men on parole. Those who attempted to hide underneath beds were pulled out by the arms, legs, and hair, then raped on the beds or floor. Pillows were used to muffle the screams. If women struggled too much, they were beaten. They were also robbed. As a result, the women fled back to prison to finish their prison terms.

Khorosho ustroitsya (to settle-in to a good place)
To be placed in a prison psychiatric institution, feigning mental illness, until the fraud is discovered.

Khryushki-prilipaly (sticking piggies)
Female petty thieves who pose as authoritative thieves in prisons where no one knows them.

Chernye barygi (black profiteers)
Convicted criminals from the Caucasus who bought fruits and vegetables from villagers and small entrepreneurs and sold them in large cities throughout Russia.

Chernye pripukhshie podnarniki (black brazen *podnarniks*; literally 'from under the bunk bed')
Petty thieves and con artists who posed as local authoritative thieves and extorted money from street vendors. When they were imprisoned and their imposture was revealed, they became prison outcasts.

Chernye reki-bespredela (black extremist racketeers)
1. Sadists who were imprisoned in northern Siberian prisons. They extorted money from their victims by torturing them with hot irons, hanging them upside down, raping them, or inserting a bottle into the vagina or anus. The old 'idealist' legitimate thieves turned them into outcasts by ordering other prisoners to forcibly sodomise them as a punishment for arrogance, conceit, and imposture. Imposture as a legitimate thief combined with extremist behaviour, tarnishes the reputation of the authoritative criminals, the old elite of the criminal world. 2. Black *mokrushnik* racketeers (i.e. those who committed murder) also become outcasts.

Terms Used to Describe Prisoners of the Gulag

BOMZHiZ: Bez Opredelennogo Mesta Zhitelstva i Zanyatiya (a homeless person)
Without an official living space or occupation, judged guilty for a breach of the passport
code according to Article 192 (1926), and Article 198 (1960), serving a sentence of one
or two years. They are not respected among the condemned, as they retain the moral and
physical characteristics of free men.

Buketniki (bouquet holders)
A male or female prisoner suffering from one or more venereal disease, such as syphilis,
chancre, the clap, etc.

Venernye stradalki (suffering Venuses)
Prostitutes, condemned for the infection of sexual partners with sexually transmitted
diseases under Article 150 (1926) and Article 115 (1960).

Glavpetuh (head cockerel)
An unofficial leader of the prison zone, he has full authority in his contact with subordinate
leaders of other unofficial groups of the ITU, and participates in the resolution of
various arguments between those falling under the jurisdiction of the 'cockerels'.

Greb v cherdachke (an oar in the attic)
A spoon poking out of the outer chest pocket of the prisoner's uniform. It signifies an
outcast prisoner (a cockerel). This symbol is strictly adhered to by the prison's rogue
authorities.

Gruzchik (a loader)
A subordinate prisoner, whom the other inmates have forced to take upon himself a crime
he didn't commit, for which there is a short sentence (for example, the murder of an
intruder to the prison zone by thieves).

Dich lagernaya (camp fowl)
Shy and withdrawn prisoners in the ITL, especially politicals, to whom, according to
inmates' law, the rogue authorities can do whatever they want: rob, beat, rape or kill.

Dokhodyaga (a goner, a famished person)
The most numerous portion of the inmates of the Gulag, weakened from starvation, broken
down through heavy labour and diseases, barely able to stand on their feet, for whom the
rogue authorities have nothing but contempt, not even considering them people.

Yebanashka (a fucked-up person)
A mentally retarded prisoner in the ITL-ITK, held in contempt.

Kolkhoz – 'Krasny Petukh' (communal farm – 'red cockerel')
A row of condemned men in the ITL-ITK, consisting entirely of the untouchables of the
prison system: cast outs, cockerels, Finns, homosexuals/passive pederasts. They are
held in separate accommodation, e.g. a barracks or bunker.

Kosyachny (a deceiver)
A prisoner who has broken the generally accepted rules of behaviour laid down by the
unofficial law of prison camp system, who for this reason has lost authority, becoming
judged, shunned, abandoned and unclean. Other prisoners are forbidden from having
relations with him, as though he were a savage.

Kurva s kotelkom (a bitch with a billycan)
A prisoner released from the camp system, who constantly carries with him a billycan
containing water. He finds scraps of food in the waste piles of the ITU, and rinses them
in the can before devouring them.

Likhie podnarniki (dashing morons)

Inmates who have committed street robberies. They are not respected by the old elite of thieves in the ITL-ITU, because they could have been victims themselves. For this reason they find themselves in a more subordinate position during their incarceration than hooligans, petty thieves, profiteers, cattle rustlers, etc.

Mama (the mother)

An unofficial leader in the prison hierarchy. Lower in status than the head cockerel.

Merzopakostnye krysy (repulsive rats)

Those convicted of hooliganism, e.g. defecating in lifts, courtyards, entry halls to blocks of flats, scrawling obscenities on the walls of houses, breaking lifts, burning and breaking postboxes and doors to blocks of flats, vandalising mansions, trees, garden benches, equipment in both children's and sporting playgrounds, breaking mirrors in houses, electric lamps, street lamps, breaking and ripping out the ear pieces of phones in public booths. All this vandalism was done in secret, without witnesses.

Miner (a mine layer)

Tried for hooliganism, e.g. the greasing with excrement of door handles to blocks of flats and flats themselves, also on the banisters of staircases and for dumping rubbish into neighbours' saucepans and kettles in a communal flat. Both men and women of the lumpen proletariat fall into this category of filth.

Mokhnoryly upyr (a shaggy-faced ghoul)

Those convicted of the rape of young children and young girls.

Mokhnoryly chert (a shaggy-faced devil)

Tried for bestial acts with minors under Articles 120 and 152 (1926).

Neprikasaemy (an untouchable)

A prisoner who has been the victim of homosexual rape by one or a group of prisoners. Morally and physically broken, they have lost human appearance, and suffer a similar status to that of a pederast. Many bestial acts are committed upon them (e.g. beating their legs). They have to carry out the filthiest menial jobs in the ITU. Other prisoners are not allowed to touch them with their hands, beating them only with their feet. It is forbidden to take or use anything belonging to them, as though they were infected. Prisoners of the camp are not allowed to give anything to them – if they did they would be beaten to death. At the table, the club and in the general running of the ITL-ITK they occupy a rear position. The administration of the ITU is forced to collect all of them into one group, to keep them in separate accommodation, have a separate place for them in the canteen, and to give them separate crockery and spoons marked with rusty holes, in order to spare them beatings, rape and murder. However, upon release from the prison camp these prisoners, to rebuild their confidence, commit the most atrocious, terrible and bloody crimes, thereby avenging their souls for years of inhuman subordination. Their victims are usually children, women and elderly people, none of whom could offer any serious resistance. One cannot pity these prisoners under any circumstances – they are guilty of the most serious crimes. If they complain the administration always answers, 'We did not invite you here; you wanted to come yourself.'

Obdristanny na portret (shit-splattered for a portrait)

Convicted from the suit of *krasnozhopye paviony* (the red-arsed baboons) they are former Communists, members of VLKSM, who have committed a crime for the second time and have consequently been sentenced to imprisonment. With the aim of demoralising them, thugs force them to sleep on the barrack floor, once the outer doors to the quarters have been closed, they defecate on their faces and clothes.

Obizhenka (the offended one)

A prisoner who has been homosexually raped or is the victim of some other type of degrading act as a punishment for breaking the unofficial laws, rules and etiquette of the prison camp system.

Obmaknuty (the baptized)

A prisoner punished by the *otritsalovka* for delinquency by slamming their head into the slop-bucket or toilet bowl. The women's *otritsalovka* performs similar acts on delinquents in the female ITL-ITK, for they are no better in their sophistication and beastliness than the men. In some cases they may even exceed the men in attempting to mock, taunt and subordinate their victims through subtle sadism.

Papa (the daddy)

An unofficial leader of a row of cells or a brigade of prisoners, including cockerels, and Finns, who is lower in rank than the head cockerel and the elder cockerel, but higher in rank than a *mama*; all these unofficial leaders are by their very nature active and passive pederasts, and as a rule they are 'combine harvesters' who have wives and children in their lives outside the camp.

Plotnik (a carpenter)

A thief who is facing expulsion from his group of rogue leaders at the command of the council of thieves, for failing to fulfil an obligation handed down by the zone authorities, or for a grave breach of prison camp thieves' law. As a result he has to commit a self-abasing act in the presence of other rogues: he is made to put a penis behind his ear, in the same way that a carpenter carries a pencil behind his ear at work.

Podmetaly-petushnya (sweeping cockerels)

A suit of untouchables in certain areas of the prison, who act as janitors in taboo places such as public toilets. They wash the floors in the barracks and the industrial zone, they sweep the ground and dig up and soften the earth in the forbidden zone, between the main compound and surrounding barbed wire fences. Participation in this kind of work is considered by the other prisoners to be beneath their status.

Podnarniki (those under a plank [bunk] bed)

Prisoners who are beaten, submissive and broken in spirit. They have been released, but for fun the guards force them to remain under a plank bed from dusk till dawn as an 'educational measure'. Such prisoners include:

Starshy petukh (the elder cockerel)

The unofficial leader of the brigade or prison row of the downcast, convicted under Article 154 (1926) and Article 121 (1960) for committing sodomy. He has inherent inclinations toward active and passive pederasty, with a track record from a young age (usually male pop artists and actors find this activity exciting; the female sex prefers lesbianism); he participates in the resolution of arguments and conflicts between the untouchables of the prison camp.

Suchka-zhuchka (little bitch)

A convicted, petty female thief, who has stolen from the personal effects of her friends in the dormitory and from the female convicts (items such as food, cigarettes, papers, matches, sugar and sweets). For this 'rattiness' she has been beaten over the head with underpants by a group of prisoners and is thereby automatically 'lowered' into the ranks of the untouchables in the female prison camp system.

Suchonka-govnoedka (the bitch shit-eater)
A big slut, a petty thief, who has been sentenced to imprisonment in the female ITL-ITK, she is spiritually and physically broken, and has had her head dunked into a toilet as a result of squabbling, spreading gossip or bad mouthing female prisoners, and is therefore 'lowered' into the ranks of the untouchables.

Suchonka-sukhodrochka (the bitch dry-masturbator)
A convicted former member of the Communist Party of the Soviet Union who is an embezzler of state and society funds.

Trakhnuty (fucked)
A mentally retarded prisoner, held in contempt by all.

Trinadtsaty otryad (the thirteenth row)
A special brigade in the zone of the ITL-ITK, consisting entirely of afflicted prisoners; such a brigade is the prison's underbelly.

Tryakhomudiya (the useless)
Prisoners without any authority, who are incapable of standing up for themselves. Somewhat mentally retarded, they hold no opinions of their own and are cowardly by nature.

'Titan' iz psikhushki (a 'Titan' from a madhouse)
A prisoner held in contempt, psychologically unstable, recuperating in the psychiatric ward of the prison hospital. He has been delivered to a place of imprisonment as a 'convalescent' to sit out his sentence.

Uzkoglazy churnyla (a slitty-eyed fool)
A prisoner of Asian descent, who is despised by the prisoners of Russian descent and the thugs and chauvinists of the ITL-ITK.

Unitaz Unitazovich Govnoedov (toilet bowl – son of toilet bowl – shit-eater)
A prisoner-*bytovik* without authority, who has had his head dunked into a toilet bowl or slop bucket full of faeces and urine.

Fantômas (Fantômas is the central character from the popular French crime novels written between 1913 and 1963, a number of which were also made into films)
A psychologically abnormal prisoner, who, instead of being imprisoned in the psychiatric hospital of the MVD prison system, is being held in the ITL-ITK.

Tselochnik (a rapist)
An afflicted prisoner, convicted of rape.

Cheburashka (a cartoon character from the 1966 children's story by Eduard Uspensky)
A despised younger passive pederast, held in the educational and work colony. He is the victim of pranks, subjugations and other revolting acts at the hands of the other younger rogue prisoners.

Chert s krasnym obosrannym khvostom (the devil with a red shitty whip)
A despised prisoner, formerly a member of the Communist Party of the Soviet Union, who has now become an 'under the plank bed victim'.

Shakalye (jackals)
Petty thief prisoners, who are 'under plank bed victims'.

Erzats (a fake)

A mentally retarded, psychologically abnormal prisoner from the camp system, who has arrived from the psychiatric hospital of the MVD after being 'cured' in order to sit out a short sentence in the prison system.

Yazychnik (a heathen)

A political prisoner convicted under the Article 58-10 (1926) for anti-Soviet agitation, who has been raped by the rogues of the prison on the orders of the NKVD-MGB. As a reward for this misdeed they received imported food products. Similar debasement and subjugation of political prisoners in the Gulag was a common occurrence.

Prevalent Diseases and Illnesses Among Prisoners of the Gulag

Main Diseases Found Among Inmates of the Gulag

Distrophy: was widespread due to chronic hunger, excessively heavy physical labour, and the general weakening of the body. It prematurely ended the lives of millions of prisoners – slaves of the Communist prison system.

Diptheria: common in corrective-labour colonies for juveniles, and more rarely in adult CLC-CLC [collective-labour colonies, collective-labour camps].

Pellagra: a skin illness caused by vitamin deficiency and constant hunger. The skin becomes uneven and rough, and covered in bloody cracks and tumours.

Syphilis: became common after the Second World War (1941–1945), originating from both local and 'brought in' sources (mainly European countries). It was able to spread through poor medical attention, and the inadequacy or complete absence of medical supplies.

Gonorrhoea: this was widespread after the Second World War among both prisoners and citizens of the free population. Before the war gonorrhoea was a rare disease in the Soviet Union.

Tuberculosis: appeared in various forms and was the scourge of all VTK, CLC-CLCs. It became significantly more common after the creation of the Communist Gulag system. This was due to chronic hunger, exhausting work, bad living conditions, over-crowding, poor medical services, and the lack of, or total absence of medicine. At the end of the 1940s and the beginning of the 1950s between thirty and thirty-five per cent of Gulag prisoners were suffering from tuberculosis, with a high mortality rate, especially in the north and Siberian corrective-labour camps and colonies.

Psychological Illnesses of Prisoners (in camp language)

Gonki (races)
A persecution mania which develops from the constant strain of the struggle for survival.

Zhor (voracious appetite)
A prisoner from the dregs of the camp, who is never full due to the systematic consumption of *balanda* (low-calorie skilly/gruel).

Zhorny/Zhornaya/-kurva s Kotletom (a person with a voracious appetite and a pot)
A prisoner from the dregs of the camp who has let himself go spiritually and physically. He constantly carries with him a jar of water, in which floats 'food' that has been found on the rubbish dump of the CLC-CLC: fish heads, skeletons with tails, potato peelings, various vegetable pieces and so on. They lick clean, 'make as smooth as plaster', the bowls from the dining hall and everything they find is consumed with a raging hunger, from which they are never free. Victims of ridicule and mockery, they are kicked for the slightest misdeed (they cannot be punched as anyone who touches them with their hands becomes 'unclean' or 'fouled' themselves).

Zhizneradostnyie (cheerful)
Prisoners in both male and female detention centres, and also corrective-labour colonies for juveniles. They do not present a danger to those around them.

Zaboboshenny (cuckoo)
A prisoner who, when deprived of freedom after his arrest, inquest and court case, constantly thinks about his family. This affects his behaviour, and his ability to fulfil

assigned work. He becomes reserved and answers questions wrongly.

Zadvinutye na Valta (obsessed with the jack/knave in playing cards)
Prisoners who, even though they are guilty, constantly think about revenge (including murder) against those who deprived them of their freedom. Victims, witnesses and those who work for police are the focus of their obsession. This condition is found in women as well as men.

Kobel-samoyed (male dog-*samoyed*)
A mentally backward prisoner-masturbator, who hangs a photograph or publication in front of himself containing an image of a woman. After achieving orgasm he eats his own sperm. They are the lowest of the low of the camp.

Shastlivye (the happy ones)
A petty bureaucrat, a Soviet man (*sovok* – person with Soviet mentality). These are psychologically damaged prisoners, who cannot comprehend or come to terms with the fact that they are in a place of detention. They are placed by the administration into inter-regional special psychiatric prison hospitals belonging to the Ministry of Internal Affairs for the USSR. This condition affects men, women, and juveniles.

U nego/neyo gus otorvalsya (his/her goose has escaped)
A mental illness among prisoners where the victim perceives everything around them to be unreal. They cannot orientate themselves in space and time, don't remember their surnames, their former address or the Article of the Criminal Code by which they have been sentenced. They confuse day and night, and do not recognise their relations.

Causes of Death in the Gulag

Death in the Gulag could be the result of any of the following: illness, incidents on site, explosions, avalanches, accidents, floods, fires, murder, inter-camp settling of scores (on the order of thieves with authority the camp administration NKGB-MGB), the suppression of strikes, uprisings, during escape attempts and torture during questioning. However inmates might die, the administration would only use the following standard medical diagnoses when listing the cause of death:
1. Acute heart attack.
2. Extensive myocardial infarction.
3. Acute kidney insufficiency.
4. Stroke.
5. Fatal liver cancer.

Places of Burial and Graves of Gulag Prisoners

1. *Ammonalnik* – a hole blasted into the permafrost.
2. Empty coal mineshafts – after the corpses were thrown in they were covered with lime chloride or rubbish and earth. The next load would then be dumped on top.
3. Individual burials – in camp cemeteries, the corpses were buried in written-off clothing, paper sacks – 'bags' and wooden coffins – 'pea jackets'.
4. Business trip/mission/into the ocean – in the northern camps of Siberia during the winter months, it was commonplace to lower naked corpses under the ice through a hole which had been cut for this purpose.

Names for Camp Cemeteries

In the language of the prisoners, camp cemeteries were called:

1. 'The Embrace of Communism.'
2. 'Into the bright future of *Sovdepiya* (the Soviet world).'
3. 'The dead-end of Socialism.'
4. 'The slag-heap of human material.'
5. 'The *Zek* sanatorium.'

The farewell phrase said to a Gulag prisoner dying of constant hunger, excessive work, illness, or killed by other prisoners was: 'Joyfully he arrived at Communism, at the bright dawn of humanity!'

Prisoner's Sadistic Games, Jokes and Entertainment

Balalaika (the balalaika)

A joke played inside the cell. When the victim is asleep, rolled up pieces of paper are placed between his fingers and set alight. The victim wakes up because of the pain, making movements with his hands similar to that of playing the balalaika.

Bashmak na dykhalku (a shoe on one's chest)

When the victim is asleep after a long day's work in the industrial zone, the *otritsaly* (members of the otritsalovka collectively) use a shoelace to tie a boot to his genitals and place it on his chest, under his chin. When the victim wakes up, he throws the shoe from his body, causing himself great pain.

Vaterpasnut (Dutch term for measuring levels, used in construction)

To drop a brick, breezeblock or other heavy object from a great hight on to a person below and then disappear. This joke is usually played from the roof or window of the work house. Occasionally this causes serious injury or death to the victim.

Vvesti narkoz (to administer anaesthetic)

To knock out the victim with a blow from a heavy object.

Velociped (the bicycle)

Similar to 'the balalaika': when the victim is asleep, rolled up pieces of paper are placed between the toes and set alight. With the rising temperature the victim wakes up, recreating the actions of pedalling a bicycle

Zapodolit poblyadushku (to pull up a slut's hem)

Played on a girl or woman, generally those belonging to the lumpen-proletariat, whose only value in male prisons are their sexual organs. Before she is gang raped, the victim's skirt or dress is lifted and tied over her head, then objects are pushed up her vagina. These may include: crushed-up empty cigarette packets, cigarette butts, matchboxes, wine bottle corks, leftover snacks, a pine cone (if in a park or forest), a large branch from a bramble bush. The intention is that the victim only realises what the items are later. This type of unpleasant situation could befall girls from decent families as well.

Igra na sakharok ili pederasta (playing for a sugar-cube or your virtue)

Cunning inmates from the *otritsalovka*, lure inexperienced inmates into a game of cards, where the price of losing can be the victim's manhood.

Mokhnushku prichastit (to baptize the cunt)

To urinate on a drunk woman's vagina after copulation.

Mena poveselit s podzharokj (to make a man laugh by frying his meat)

A way of extorting money and other things of value. The body is burnt with an electric iron, and an electrode is pushed into the victim's anus.

Opustit vtikhouyu (to lower quietly)

One of the most despicable acts of humiliation used on urban convicts by convicted hoodlums from the *otritsalovka*. A physically strong grown man, of solid character, who is unaware of the authority of the other convicts, would have a convict's penis (or a rag soaked in sperm or vaginal fluids), wiped across his lips at night when he is sleeping. This is done in the presence of a group of 'witnesses' with the intention of 'lowering' the victim into the cast of the fallen or downcast. Women would be 'lowered' into the class of whores and pigs.

Podlyanshiki krysy i krysyata (leaders of the rats and baby rats)

An initiation rite that takes place in a large block of flats. The lifts must be broken then defecated in, and faeces must be smeared on the door handles of all flats and the block's main entrance. Faeces must be left in all the flower boxes and hallways. Broken glass from the windows is scattered on the first and second floors. The entrances and doors to the flats are set on fire, the locks are broken and the electric doorcode destroyed. Everything is graffitied, all the lights are broken, the postboxes are burnt, the rubbish and bins are set alight, any rubbish skips are beaten out of shape. All benches are broken, all facilities such as playgrounds or sports areas are also destroyed, trees are cut down and plants uprooted. Any pigeons, cats or dogs found in the area are captured, tortured and killed. This type of initiation is carried out by homeless children, children with a troubled history (who attend special schools), children who are underage offenders and recent inmates of child correctional colonies.

Pogladit ruchnikom po tykve (to stroke the pumpkin)
To corral the victim into a doorway or park with the intention of robbing them. The victim is hit on the head with a hammer, her earrings are stolen, along with any other valuable items that can be found in the victim's handbag.

Poteshitsya (to have fun)
A sadistic game carried out after the rape of a woman, whereby her genitalia are poked with a broom or any other bristly object at hand.

Prichastit kosmocha za grev (to take communion for a parcel)
To forcefully sodomise a member of the clergy, with the objective of humiliating the victim. Carried out on the orders of the NKVD-MGB, afterwards the rapist would be rewarded with food or cigarettes by the authorities in gratitude for this act.

Rekratsukha bychkov i telok (recreation with bulls and calves)
To take a hostage for ransom.

Seans dat (to give a show)
With the intention of causing mischief, the perpetrator has sexual intercourse with a drunk woman in front of a large crowd of people. Her legs are lifted high and the man sings various rude verses.

Soedinit Volgu s Donom (to connect the Volga to the Don)
A form of sadistic rape, whereby the vaginal crevice and anal cavity are stretched together using one's fingers, ignoring the protests of the victim.

Spustit podlyanku na podlyanku (to trick a trickster)
To goad three groups of convicts into fighting for a joke, then make peace.

Surpriz-mina (the surprise mine)
To defecate in the flat one is robbing, the faeces are then concealed for the owner of the apartment to discover later.

Upyr mokhnoryly (the mossy ghoul)
The condemnation of paedophiles and those who brutally and viciously rape women. In one case a criminal stretched the orifices of his victims for his own amusement, and to give them something to remember him by. The nature of the man's crimes were made known to the staff and inmates at the prison he was sent to, so that the inmates could fully understand 'who is who' and carry out their own form of justice.

Shlyumku nadryuchit na kumpol (to put a bowl on the crown)
Practised in order to humiliate the victim and amuse the perpetrators. A full bowl of prison gruel is emptied over the head of a randomly selected victim.

Shutka (the joke: sadistic recreational acts)
1: To pour petrol or kerosene over an unsuspecting sleeping convict and set fire to him. Usually the petrol was only poured onto the lower half of the body. 2: To hammer a nail through the victims stool or bench. 3: To urinate or pour acid into the victim's water jug. 4: To spread axle grease over a bench, or to cover the floor around it with ball-bearings. 5: To place a large breezeblock above a door, so when it is opened the block falls directly onto the victim's head. 6: To place excrement inside the bread ration. 7: To place a lighted cigarette inside the victim's jacket pocket. 8: To attach an electrode to a metal door handle. 9: To defecate into an unsuspecting convict's shoes during the night.

Shutka chernozhopykh i zheltomordykh zverey (a joke played on black-arsed and yellow-faced beasts)
Carried out on those of Circassian or Asian origins. The victim was castrated and his testicles were stuffed in his mouth, he was then forced to swallow them, nearly choking in the process. The attackers did not kill him so that when they were caught, they would receive a lighter sentence.

Erzats-estradnik (a phoney performer)
As a joke and a form of exhibitionism, the perpetrator exposes his genitalia to women and young children (especially girls). Accompanied with rude gestures.

Yaponskoye/Gruzinskoye tango (the Japanese/Georgian tango)
A form of sadistic recreation and a method of settling disputes between *blatnye*. Two blindfolded convicts fight each other with knives of identical size and length, surrounded by completely silent inmates. The first serious drawing of blood decides the fight. After the tango all sins and debts are forgiven. A display of courage like this was reserved for *blatnye* only.

Terms Used to Describe the Actions of the Prison System Administration

Avtoruchka, list bumagi ili kher v ochko? (a pen, a piece of paper or a cock up the arse?)
The offer made to a thief by the authorities to compel him into renouncing the thieves' world. If he refused he was placed in a *khata* (pressing cell) where pressers (see page 213) would torture and anally rape him 'in chorus', until he agreed to abandon his thieving ways.

Aktivny raskol (rigorous interrogation)
An interrogation where the victim was beaten up and water poured over him every time he lost consciousness.

Baranyee kresty (ram's crosses)
This system of marking a convict's file began in 1947. Following the repeal of the death penalty for murder, the camp court would only add a twenty-five year sentence for this crime, leading to a dramatic increase in murders among convicts. Red pencil crosses were marked in the personal file of any prisoner who killed in this way. Some convicted thieves had over ten crosses; their victims were usually politicals.

Bely Lebed ITU (the White Swan Prison)
The conditions created by the administration at this prison, were particularly cruel. Inmates were suppressed and subjected to intense physiological pressure. Even an authoritative 'thief in law' could be raped or lowered in other ways.

Bez poslednego (minus the last one)
The methodical execution of prisoners by firing squad, after the order *Vykhodi na rabotu* (come out to work). To discourage lingering in the barracks the last convict to line up for work after this command would be taken beyond the guarded zone and executed.

Birka zeka (a convict's label)
Before dead convicts were allowed to be buried, a piece of plywood or hard piece of card measuring no more than 6 by 8 centimetres would be tied to the big toe of the body using wire or twine. The label would carry the details of the inmate, written with a lead pencil. The graphite of the pencil would keep well in the soil, in the event of future exhumation.

Bich otlovlenny dlya scheta (citizens caught for the quota)
A number of convicts would escape from every Gulag convoy. To make up the balance vagrants were caught at railway stations and press-ganged into the carriages. On arrival at the ITL these innocent citizens would be given over to the system, despite their protests. It might take years before the 'mistake' was officially recognised. Even then it was often less trouble for the authorities to keep these 'suspects' rather than let them out.

Bolty v khezalnik ili avtoruchka i bumaga? (a bolt [cock] in the arse or a pen and paper?)
The offer made to *blatnye otritsaly* (prisoners who refuse to submit to the prison rules). They were forced to write a text renouncing their criminal life then read it over the zone's public announcement system. It would tell of their 'wish to step on the path to correction and work, and to be of use to society'. If they refused they were placed into a *khata* (pressing cell) where they would be beaten and raped.

Bumerang (the boomerang)
To discourage complaints from the convicts, any allegations made about a specific employee of the ITU were delt with by the same employee.

V stoylo zagnat ili otritsalu vydat zamuzh (into the cowshed or to marry off an *otritsala*, i.e a member of the *otritsalokva*)
Anyone who breaks the regime and refused to work, would be placed in a special cell where

he'd be beaten up and raped under the instructions of the administration.

Zabytye (the forgotten ones)

Citizens were sometimes arrested by the NKVD-MVD without official orders and placed in over-crowded cells with those who had already been sentenced. When the time came to transfer the prisoners to the Gulag everyone in the cell was transported, including those without official orders. Once they reached the camp they would only be freed with much difficulty, often after months or years had passed.

Zadelat paskhalnogo gusya (to make an Easter goose)

A recidivist thief would be placed in a pressing cell, tied into a mattress cover and hung up for hours or even days. He would have no option but to urinate and defecate in his clothes. After being allowed out of the cover to eat, he was rehung. This was an effective method of making the thief renounce the criminal authorities. Following this torture they would put his excrement-covered trousers on his head and place him in a cell of thieves.

Zadelat paskhalnogo gusya s rikhtovkoy (to flatten an Easter goose)

A recidivist thief was placed in a pressing cell with a gag in his mouth, where he was tied in a mattress cover and laid on the floor. There he would be beaten with broomhandles and kicked. During this beating his persecutors demand that he renounce the thieves clan, then they release him from the cover. If he refuses to renounce they replace it and continue beating him until they get a positive result.

Zatknut klyap (to plug with a gag)

When a condemned convict is taken from his cell to be shot, a special soft gag is used which has straps similar to those of a gas mask. This prevents him from screaming.

Zonu zaglushit (to suppress the zone)

The administration would take all the *otritsaly* (including their leaders, who had a hostile attitude to the camp regime), out of the ITK, and transport them to camps in the distant northern tundra and Siberian forest. This would help secure order and discipline among the remaining convicts by controlling the regime, reinforcing re-education and improving the productivity of their labour in the industrial zone.

Zonu slomat (to break the zone)

Special forces of the MVD would enter the zone to bring the regime to order, usually where the inmates had rebelled against the despotism of the thieves, who had been ruling over them. They would pick out the *blatnye* who had deliberately 'defrosted' the zone, provoking riots, and take them to the pre-trial detention centre. There they would be sentenced to between eight and fifteen years imprisonment or the death penalty, then transferred to other prison regime camps in distant northern and Siberian areas.

Klassovy podkhod (class attitude)

The protective attitude of the law enforcement agencies toward the nomenclatura who stole state and communal property.

Koridor ognevoy (fire corridor)

The forbidden zone was surrounded by barbed wire (during the winter months the snow wasn't removed from this area, in summer the ground was raked over). This zone was alarmed, and in the dark it would be lit with electric lamps and spotlights. The main fence was painted white, both inside and out, to make it easier to see escapees. Guards had the right to shoot to kill anyone entering this area.

Lokalnaya vyshka (watchtower)

A tower where during the day a convict activist would be on duty, keeping an eye on the camp, making sure order is observed. He would have a local telephone connected to the reception desk, the checkpoint (KPP) and the assistant head of the camp on duty (DPNK) as well as the head office of the ITK.

Matsatka (a forty gallon barrel)
A form of execution by the VChK. The victim was placed into a barrel lined with sharp nails which was then rolled around until he was dead. When removed from the barrel the body would be almost completely drained of blood.

Metodom leninskogo phizicheskogo ubezhdeniya (the Lenin method of physical persuasion)
Interrogation with sadistic tortures using instruments and technical means.

Na zapretku vygnat (to send onto the forbidden zone)
To make the newly arrived convicts work constructing the forbidden zone. They would place the barbed wire, paint the fence white and dig the ground. This work was considered to be *zapadlo* (beneath their dignity) by the other convicts. For the administration it was an effective method of discovering the *otritsaly* among the newly arrived. They were placed in SHIZO (solitary confinement) for refusing this type of work, and marked out by the administration as potential breakers of the ITL regime in the future.

Na porevo prodat kuratku-chukhnu (to sell a girl from the Baltic states)
Thieves, who had already bought girls from the NKVD during their transportation to the Gulag, would then sell these (political) girls from the Baltics to other criminals for money or goods. These transactions would take place on the way to eastern Siberia or Komi-ASSR. The thieves law allowed her new owner to strangle or stab the girl if she did anything wrong, to give her up to satisfy the sexual needs of other convicts in the carriage or to sell her as a slave to another criminal. The guard would have already written her off as dead on the journey (among political prisoners the death rate was very high). Beautiful young girls from the Baltic states were more valuable than those from western Ukraine and Modolvia. This trade was very common in the1940s.

NKVDevsky bespredel KPSS (the excesses of the NKVD of the Communist Party)
The various methods of taking away a person's humanity in the Gulag through hunger, humiliation, torture, beatings, spiritual and physical suppression with the real threat to health and life. All these methods were legitimised by the Communist ideology of the elimination of enemies.

Obvalka (dissection)
After executions in prison, the corpses were chopped up using butchers' axes, the body parts would then be placed into a powerful electric cutter. The resulting 'minced meat' was mixed with the prison sewage, put through the treatment plant, then disposed of in canals, ditches and rivers.

Obvinilovka s gruzom (indictment with burden)
Convicts who were suffering from drug addiction and alcoholism were additionally sentenced to forced treatment at the ITU, where they would serve their term until both the medical commission and the court decided to release them. No amnesty, free pardon or release on parole was applied to such prisoners.

Oblomnaya kamera (the breaking cell)
A special prison cell where, on the orders of the administration, the prisoners (including politicals), were 'firmly put on the road to correction' using 'the methods of physical

persuasion': tortures, beatings and the rape of both men and women.

Perdilnik (the farting room)

A special 'freezer cell' in the prison, a SHIZO without glass (only bars) in the window, where the temperature is the same as in the guarded zone outside. Ferocious *otritsaly*, authoritative thieves, and politicals were placed here wearing nothing but their underwear, for two to three hours, in temperatures up to twenty-five degrees below freezing. The aim of this punishment was re-education.

Petushinaya Uralskaya zona (cockerel's Ural zone)

The MVD set up an experimental colony where they brought inmates who had been 'lowered' from different ITKs across the country with the intention of saving them from discrimination, torture, beatings and rape. It was in this colony that the slaves of the slaves showed what they were capable of. The cruellest settling of scores began, with murders, stabbings, rapes and tortures. They fought for leadership of the zone according to where they came from, their crimes etc. The colony turned into the worst hell on earth.

Pod koromyslo musorov popast (to end up under the yoke of rubbish)

A method of punishing a convict breaker of the regime who had assaulted guards. They were handcuffed yoke backwards, with one arm over the shoulder and the other round the side, so the wrists met behind the back. Sometimes they would be hung on a hook by the elbow. The convict would scream in severe pain, soil himself, and after a short period, lose consciousness. (This NKVD method was later used by the Gestapo and SS.)

Pod naporom rabota (working under pressure)

1. This absurd prison camp socialist competition was invented by the Communists. The criminals (hooligans, thieves, robbers, killers, rapists), and their brigades would be awarded the first, second and third places, and handed red pennants displaying texts about raising productivity and portraits of Lenin. 2. Such socialist competition particularly raged in pressing cells where, as a warning, those who did not fulfil the norm would be repeatedly hit on the head. If that didn't work, the other convicts in the cell (the whole brigade), would beat them. There were no lazy or depressed inmates in such cells, as they would be beaten too. Everyone was smiling, working with enthusiasm and performing over and above target, this was the 'Dawn of Communism' – in a prison cell...

Pravo pervoy nochi khozyaina (the master's right of the first night)

On arriving at the distant women's Siberian or northern Gulag ITL of the NKVD-NVD, groups of wives and daughters of 'enemies of the people' would go through a medical examination where the authorities picked out the most beautiful, slender, virgin girls. The lustful head of the camp would then be informed of the selection. According to unwritten camp law, he had the 'right of the first night' – to sleep with the convict slaves of the Communist system. He would choose a girl that he liked and call her to his office, where he would ask her to become his mistress; in exchange she would receive privileges. Any girl who refused would simply be raped and sent to the hardest labour sites: logging, constructing log rafts (where they would have to stand in freezing water up to their necks), loading logs onto trains and barges, as well as bricks, sacks of cement etc., or they would be put into the SHIZO, to break them spiritually. Some of these desecrated girls would commit suicide because of these conditions.

Pravo pervomu slomat ochko (the right to be the first to break the arse)

The authoritative criminal of the pressing cell would be the first to rape the victim who had been placed there by the administration of the ITU, NKGB-MGB (the victims were *otritsaly*, authoritative criminals, legitimate thieves, those who refused to work and politicals). The other pressing cell inmates would then rape the victim in the order of status established by the authoritative criminal in charge of the cell.

Pressovshchik (coerced operator)

A special executioner/torturer who was recruited from the criminals of the lumpen proletariat or the fringes of society. Kept in special cells, they were exempted from hard labour, given plentiful rations taken from other prisoners' personal parcels and provided with alcohol. They followed the orders of the camp authorities to rape, beat and break the spirit of other inmates, with the intention of stopping their life of crime, and to ensure they led a normal life in the future. Their victims included professional criminals, habitual criminals, robbers, politicals, perpetrators of armed attacks, malicious saboteurs of the camp regime, women and children, racketeers and murderers.

Raskol tretey stepeni (third degree interrogation)

An interrogation using torture and special instruments to make the victim admit to any absurd accusation, e.g. spying for bourgeois states such as Antarctica, Mont Blanc, Vesuvius, Euphrates, Bosphorus, Sierra Nevada, Atlantic etc. Especially popular during the period 1937 to 1939, when NKVD cadets on practical training in Siberia or the Near East amused themselves by beating confessions out of semi-literate peasants. They created a situation where the more 'saboteurs' and 'enemies of the people' they found, the more capable they were proved. There was even competition between cities and regions (Vladivostok and Khabarovsk, Novosibirsk and Kemerovo, Sverdlovsk and Chelyabinsk, Moscow and Leningrad, etc.). At the tribunals and special meetings where they were tried, many of these semi-literate peasants could not even articulate the name of the 'bourgeois state' supposedly employing them to 'spy', or carry out 'sabotage'. This elicited only smiles from the iniquitous Communist 'judge'-executioners.

Skvoz stroy kozlov i opushchennykh (through a line of bastards and lesser criminals)

Newly admitted dangerous criminals were forced between two lines of inmates who, for whatever reason, felt negatively toward professional criminals. The new admission was beaten with rubber truncheons prior to being allocated a cell. As is well known, professional criminals generally come from the fringes of society and the lumpen proletariat, and respect only rough physical force involving actual threat to life and limb. Decades of experience taught camp administrations that words were useless and only physical force had any effect. This was condemned by humanitarians and democrats who never experienced the brutality and parasitism these criminals displayed. The laws of the criminal world are based on fear, blood and death – just like those of the Communist system. Such brutal measures were designed to kill all desire in the criminals to oppose the camp regime, or to reject undertaking labour for the benefit of the society in which they were formerly parasites.

Slomat krytuyu (break the cover)

The correctional labour camp used violence and force to destroy the psychology of the criminals and their 'romanticism'. Habitual criminals who were against the camp regime and its work requirements were subject to harsh corrective measures to make them renounce the world of crime and introduce them to socially useful labour. To achieve the desired results these measures were taken without pity or compassion. In the event of mass insubordination, Spetsnaz (from the Ministry of the Interior) was called upon.

Sotslyut (social-ferocious)

1. An orphanage for abandoned children. 2. Pupils of special schools for difficult children from troubled backgrounds. 3. A special technical college for the children of criminals, vagrants and the poor. 4. A corrective labour camp system with a general regime where first-time criminals were held before being sent to their final camp. All kinds of minor criminals who joined the fight for leadership in the camp were held here. As a result, many fights broke out between the different groups and grew into large, chaotic arguments with no rules or criminal etiquette, only rape, mutilation, and murder. The most violent offenders were those under the age of eighteen who had already been in young offenders' institutions and were later transferred to adult camps. These young people with their love of disorder were a permanent group of troublemakers in all adult camps.

Spetsnaz MVD rikhtovka (Ministry of the Interior Spetsnaz 'fixers')

Suppressors of mutiny and mass insubordination of convicted criminals in the corrective labour camp system. Criminals who carried out arson attacks on the camp were dispersed with water canon, and the main perpetrators segregated for trial under Article 77 of the Soviet Criminal Code (1960) for the disruption of corrective labour institutions. This crime carried a prison sentence of between eight to fifteen years or the death penalty. Article 321 of the current Russian Criminal Code (1996) punishes the same crimes with prison sentences of between five to twelve years.

Stoyka mordoy v ugol, ruki po shvam (to face the corner, arms by your sides)

A brazier which burns for many hours, in which the legs of prisoners are burnt and swollen. Implemented in certain prison camps, this practise originates from interrogation methods employed by organs such as the NKVD, NKGB and MGB in the 1930s and 1940s.

Tverdo vstavshy na put ispravleniya (firmly put upon the path toward correction)

1. A prisoner, who has refused to become involved in crime and has ceased criminal activity. 2. Someone who has become an active and willing assistant to the MVD and KGB. 3. Someone who has become involved in the internal routine/order section (SVP), to help the administration in the prison zones. 4. Someone who has become an enforcer for the authorities, helping them remove the seasoned criminals and thieves, along with their laws which use homosexual rape, torture, beatings and debasement as punishments.

Tramvay (a tram)

A special place in the prison camp, where prisoners convicted of particularly cruel and bloody crimes gang-rape girls and women who are considered 'harmful' and 'enemies of the people', with the aim of coercing them into giving necessary information to the NKVD-NKGB-MGB. Having chosen their victims from among the prisoners, the authorities ask them mockingly, 'Are you happy being a sex slave? Your male cellmates are very satisfied with you, and have asked that you be left in their cell a little longer. Do you want to go and meet them now? Or shall we continue the talks we started earlier...' and so on. Only those strong in character can withstand such inhumane subjugations. The inmate-'tram drivers' were not allowed to beat these unfortunate girls and women, only to rape them, force them to have oral sex and to stick their fingers inside their vaginas. After the testimony/confession 'in the tram' of around twenty victims, all the convicts shot themselves, helping to preserve the secret of these terrible methods of investigation.

Tryum (the ship's hold)

A special torture cell used for the interrogation of 'enemies of the people'. Rats were kept in a special container, on top of which both men and women were seated without their underwear. The bottom of the container would then be heated with a kerosene lamp, causing the rats to try to escape by jumping up and biting into the victim's body. Men's testicles were specially tied up and positioned to aid the torture process. The rats were kept in metal cages in the holding cells, their legs chained to prevent them escaping. Rats were the first helpers of the NKVD-NKGB-MGB and the 'armed forces of the party'; such interrogations were considered highly effective.

Uboyny tsekh (the workshop of death)
A building or place, where death sentences are carried out by liquidators during 'bloody' days, nights and 24 hour periods, approved by committees, tribunals and courts.

Uzda musorov (a pig's [police] bridle)
To put a straight jacket on a prisoner who has broken the prison regime, or who has attacked a member of the administration regime. The legs of the convict would be bent backwards so that they nearly touch the convict's own neck and a strap is put across his mouth. The back cramps up completely while the inmate is lying on his stomach, either on the cell floor or in the corridor. This constricting position causes the victim to lose consciousness in about thirty minutes. Prisoners who have experienced this 'curbing of the filth', when threatened with a straight jacket by the administration of the ITU or with punishment from the elders in their prison block, quickly understand the consequences and say, 'Boss, forgive me, I'll put a cork in it...' or something similar.

Chernaya Marusya (the Black Maria)
A truck or saloon car belonging to the organs of the NKVD-MGB used for the transportation of arrested men and convicts. It is equipped with a 'glass' compartment for one person and an observation aperture or 'top'. Usually they were disguised with a sign on the side reading 'Bread', 'Vegetables', etc. Very rarely they were painted with the threatening initials 'NKVD'. Commonly referred to as 'the Black Crow' or 'the Black Maria' people were frightened of these vehicles and avoided them at all costs.

Sharashki (secret buildings)
Special secret engineering bureaus and laboratories within the Gulag system where highly qualified convicts and 'enemies of the people' (academics, doctors and PhD students, engineers, constructors and workers), carry out work that is military, strategic and tactical in nature. They are organised by the KPSS, and have a headquarters in Moscow.

Shlyuza (sluice)
The twin gates in the KPP (checkpoint), which open in turn to allow vehicles through. Here, with the aid of specially trained dogs, all vehicles are searched for prisoners attempting to escape from the ITU, as well as weapons, contraband, drugs and spirits.

Shtrafnik po nakatu gebeshnikov (fined for assaulting KGB officers)
A dissident political prisoner, convicted by the administration of the ITU for breaking the laws of imprisonment by starting fights, keeping drugs, pornographic images, banknotes or spirits, either by hiding them under their beds or by sewing them into their pockets. They are placed in SHIZO (solitary confinement), preventing them from early release for good behaviour, or as part of the work programme for 'houses for the people'.

Eshelonka (echelon)
Internal convoy regiments of the NKVD-MVD who escort prisoners from one prison camp to another according to their documents.

Bibliography

Martin Amis, *Koba the Dread*, 2002
Anne Applebaum, *Gulag: A History*, 2003
Danzig Baldaev, *Russian Criminal Tattoo Encyclopaedia Volume I, II, III*, 2003-2008
Janusz Bardach (with Kathleen Gleeson), *Man Is Wolf To Man: Surviving Stalin's Gulag*, 1998
Martin J. Bollinger, *Stalin's Slave Ships*, 2003
Edward Buca, *Vorkuta*, 1976
Reader Bullard, *Inside Stalin's Russia: The Diaries of Reader Bullard 1930-1934*, 2000, (edited by Julian and Margaret Bullard)
Robert Conquest, *The Great Terror: A Reassessment*, 1990
Robert Conquest, *The Harvest of Sorrow: Soviet Collectivization and the Terror-Famine*, 1986
Miriam Dobson, *Khrushchev's Cold Summer*, 2009
Meyer Galler and Harlan E. Marquess, *Soviet Prison Camp Speech*, 1972
Evgeniya Ginzburg, *Journey into the Wirldwind*, 1967
Catriona Kelly, *Comrade Pavlik: The Rise and Fall of a Soviet Boy Hero*, 2005
Edward Kuznetsov, *Prison Diaries*, 1975
Nadezhda Mandelstam, *Hope Against Hope*, 1999
Anatoly Marchenko, *My Testimony*, 1969
Vladimir Petrov, *It Happens In Russia: Seven Years Forced Labour in the Siberian Goldfields*, 1951
Irina Ratushinskaya, *No, I'm Not Afraid*, 1986
Varlam Shalamov, *Kolyma Tales*, 1980
Michael Solomon, *Magadan*, 1971
Aleksandr Solzhenitsyn, *The Gulag Archipelago*, 1973
Leona Toker, *Return from the Archipelago*, 2000
Hava Volovich, *Till My Tale Is Told: Women's Memoirs of the Gulag*, 2001, (edited by Simeon Vilensky)

Further information:
fuel-design.com/russian-criminal-tattoo-archive

Russian Criminal Tattoo Encyclopaedia Volume I
Danzig Baldaev and Sergei Vasiliev

Russian Criminal Tattoo Encyclopaedia Volume II
Danzig Baldaev and Sergei Vasiliev

Russian Criminal Tattoo Encyclopaedia Volume III
Danzig Baldaev and Sergei Vasiliev

Soviets
Danzig Baldaev and Sergei Vasiliev

Russian Criminal Tattoo Police Files Volume I
Arkady Bronnikov

Russian Criminal Tattoos and Playing Cards
Arkady Bronnikov

First published in 2010
Reprinted in 2013, 2019, 2021

Murray & Sorrell FUEL Ltd
FUEL Design & Publishing
33 Fournier Street
London E1 6QE

www.fuel-design.com

Special thanks to: Valentina Baldaeva

The publishers would especially like to thank the
following people for generously giving their time
and expertise:
Margarita Baskakova, Anna Benn, Clementine
Cecil, Tina Colquhoun, Julia Dvinskaya, Julia
Goumen, Ast A. Moore, Ralph Pickering, Richard
Pickering, Rebecca Warren.

Translation: www.GMTranslations.com

Distribution by Thames & Hudson / D. A. P.
ISBN: 978-0-9563562-4-6
Printed in Singapore